Beginning the Five-String Banjo

Beginning the Five-String Banjo

JERRY SILVERMAN

74-138

Macmillan Publishing Co., Inc.

New York

Collier Macmillan Publishers

London

Macmillan Publishing Co., Inc.
866 Third Avenue, New York, N. Y. 10022
Collier-Macmillan Canada Ltd.,

First Printing 1974

Printed in the United States of America

Library of Congress Cataloging in Publication Data
Silverman, Jerry.
    Beginning the five-string banjo.

    1. Banjo—Methods—Self instruction.
I. Title.
MT568.S57   787'.7'0712   73-5288

CONTENTS

Beginning the Five-String Banjo

CHAPTER ONE

BASICS

First Things First

Trim the fingernails of your left hand as short as possible. Trim the nails on your right hand to about one-eighth inch. Don't mind the asymmetrical appearance—after all, you are about to become a very special person—a *banjo player!*

Now that you have completed your manicure, hold your hands up before you like this:

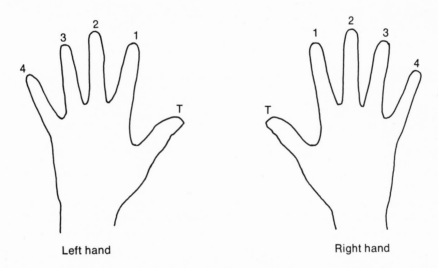

Left hand   Right hand

The fingers are numbered 1 through 4 starting with the index finger. The thumbs are not numbered but always referred to as "thumbs."

The banjo may be played either in a standing or seated position. You had best be seated for your studies. You may stand at your debut recital if you wish.

The left hand supports the neck of the banjo. The left thumb is used as a counterpressure to the fingers, along the back of the neck. The left hand's fingers press down on the strings; that is, the fingertips—and that's why we need short nails.

The fingers of the right hand (including the thumb) strike the strings in a variety of ways.

Now let's look at the banjo itself.

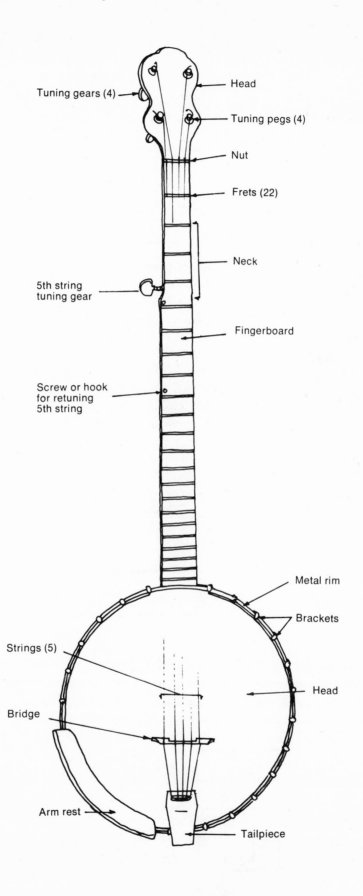

Tuning gears (4)

Head

Tuning pegs (4)

Nut

Frets (22)

Neck

5th string
tuning gear

Fingerboard

Screw or hook
for retuning
5th string

Metal rim

Brackets

Strings (5)

Head

Bridge

Arm rest

Tailpiece

Let's take a closer look at the first few frets.

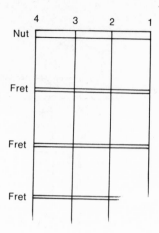

Using this bird's-eye view we can construct simple diagrams to show you where to put the fingers of your left hand to play *chords*. All we have to do is put little numbered dots on the desired strings at the proper frets and you will be able to see at a glance where to go. But first . . .

The G Tuning

Unlike most musical instruments, the five-string banjo does not have a fixed tuning. Depending upon the circumstances, the strings are tuned to a variety of notes. The whys and wherefores of these various tunings we will go into anon. Suffice it to say that the easiest tuning to begin with is the *G tuning*.

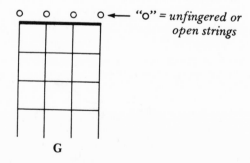

If you strike all the strings *open*—that is, unfingered by the left hand—you will get a *G major chord* (referred to simply as "G" from here on out).

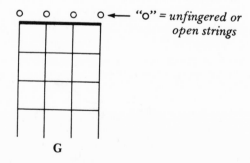

The Nail-Brush

Brush down over the first four strings (don't hit the fifth) with the nails of fingers 2, 3, and 4 of your right hand. The movement should be quick and decisive, like shaking down a thermometer.

Musically it is written like this:

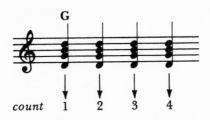

or simply

Now let's try a chord which needs to be fingered by the left hand: *D7.*

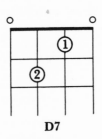

D7

You will see from the diagram that the first finger presses near the first fret (we say "at the first fret") of the second string. The second finger presses at the second fret of the third string. Press as close to the frets as possible without actually touching them. The strings must remain in firm contact with the frets while the chord is being played.

Here's a simple exercise to practice:

Play G (open) four times slowly: 1-2-3-4
Play D7 four times slowly: 1-2-3-4
Play G four times slowly: 1-2-3-4
Play D7 four times slowly: 1-2-3-4

Now you are ready for your first song. Begin playing G slowly before you start to sing. (Always start playing before you start to sing. That will give you the right first note and set the general mood of the piece.)

Skip to My Lou

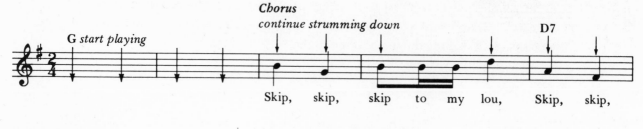

G	G
I'll get another one prettier than you,	Flies in the buttermilk, shoo fly shoo,
D7	**D7**
I'll get another one prettier than you,	Flies in the buttermilk, shoo fly shoo,
G	**G**
I'll get another one prettier than you,	Flies in the buttermilk, shoo fly shoo,
D7 ___ **G**	**D7** ___ **G**
Skip to my lou, my darling. *Chorus*	Skip to my lou, my darling. *Chorus*
G	**G**
Little red wagon painted blue,	Gone again, skip to my lou,
D7	**D7**
Little red wagon painted blue,	Gone again, skip to my lou,
G	**G**
Little red wagon painted blue,	Gone again, skip to my lou,
D7 ___ **G**	**D7** ___ **G**
Skip to my lou, my darling. *Chorus*	Skip to my lou, my darling. *Chorus*

That was easy, wasn't it? Now let's learn a third chord, *C*. Most folk songs can be accompanied with these three chords.

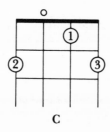

C

She'll Be Comin' 'Round the Mountain

This note (B) is not playable on the banjo.

comes,   She'll be com - in' 'round the moun - tain when she comes,   She'll be

com - in' 'round the moun - tain, she'll be com - in' 'round the moun - tain, She'll be

com - in' 'round the moun - tain when she comes.

                 G
She'll be riding six white horses when she comes,

                                   D7
She'll be riding six white horses when she comes,

                 G   C
She'll be riding six white horses, she'll be riding six white horses,

               D7   G
She'll be riding six white horses when she comes.

                 G
She'll be wearing pink pajamas when she comes,

                                   D7
She'll be wearing pink pajamas when she comes,

                 G   C
She'll be wearing pink pajamas, she'll be wearing pink pajamas,

               D7   G
She'll be wearing pink pajamas when she comes.

                 G
Oh, we'll all go out to meet her when she comes,

                                   D7
Oh, we'll all go out to meet her when she comes,

                 G   C
Oh, we'll all go out to meet her and we'll all go out to greet her,

               D7   G
Oh, we'll all go out to meet her when she comes.

                 G
Oh, we'll kill the old red rooster when she comes,

                                   D7
Oh, we'll kill the old red rooster when she comes,

                 G   C
Oh, we'll kill the old red rooster, 'cause he don't crow like he useter,

               D7   G
Oh, we'll kill the old red rooster when she comes.

The Ups and Downs—A Little Rhythm

Instead of playing an endless series of downstroke nail-brushes, we will now divide the basic beat in two, as follows:

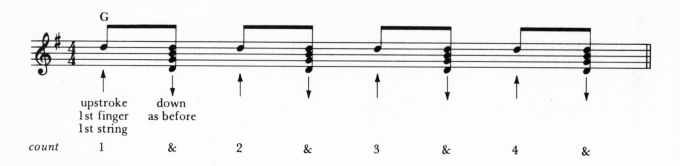

The first finger may strike any of the four strings on its way up. It may also alternate between any two strings or play a pattern involving three or four strings.

Gee, But I Wanna Go Home

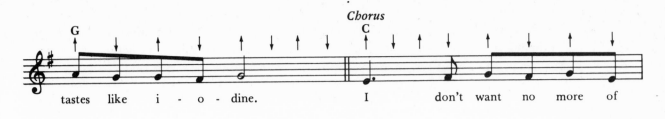

tastes like i - o - dine. I don't want no more of

ar - my life, Gee, but I wan - na go home. _____

G   D7
The biscuits that they give you, they say are mighty fine;

                    G
One rolled off a table and it killed a pal of mine. *Chorus*

                    G   D7
The chickens that they give you, they say are mighty fine;

                    G
One rolled off a table and it started marking time. *Chorus*

                    G   D7
The details that they give us, they say are mighty fine;

                    G
The garbage that we pick up they feed us all the time. *Chorus*

                    G   D7
The clothes that they give you, they say are mighty fine;

                    G
But me and my buddy can both fit into mine. *Chorus*

                    G   D7
The women in the service club, they say are mighty fine;

                    G
But most are over ninety and the rest are under nine. *Chorus*

                    G   D7
They treat us all like monkeys and make us stand on line;

                    G
They give us fifty dollars and take back forty-nine. *Chorus*

The Real Thing—Wherein the Thumb Gets into the Act and Produceth
★★★ *The Basic Banjo Strum* ★★★

You've probably been wondering what the fifth string is doing halfway up the neck of the banjo, all by its lonesome, seemingly neglected by both hands. Well, wonder no more. It is your right thumb which now enters the fray and combines with the nail-brush downstroke to produce the all-purpose basic banjo strum.

9

The thumb does not move independently (as in playing the guitar, for example). It moves downward only as the wrist moves downward in effecting the nail-brush. About two inches separate the thumb from the index finger.

This distance does not change significantly as the nails brush over the strings and the thumb, following along, comes into contact with the fifth string.

Important: As the thumb moves downward toward its rendezvous with the fifth string, it first comes into contact with the head of the banjo about an inch or so above the fifth string. It then slides along the head until it is stopped momentarily by the fifth string. Its downward course then continues and it plucks the fifth string.

It might be a good idea to draw a light pencil line on the head of your banjo about an inch above the fifth string as a target for your thumb.

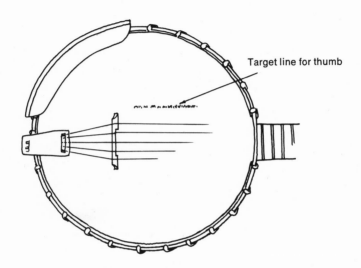

Target line for thumb

Now you are ready for a simple exercise which will lead you directly to the basic banjo strum.

basic downstroke   thumb 5th string

The strum is completed by adding the upstroke with the index finger before the nail-brush thumb combination.

up   down   thumb

count	1	&	uh	2	&	uh	3	&	uh	4	&	uh
or say	bump	dit	- ty	bump	dit	- ty	bump	dit	- ty	bump	dit	- ty

If your thumb seems to get caught by the fifth string because in sliding it along the head it hits the underside of the string, a small carpentry job is in order. You will have to deepen the notch on the bridge in which the fifth string is resting. This can be done with a small v-shaped file or a penknife. Be *very* careful not to gouge too deeply or the string will wind up too low and then you'll really be in trouble.

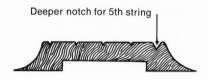

Now let's go back and try the strum again. This time try switching from chord to chord.

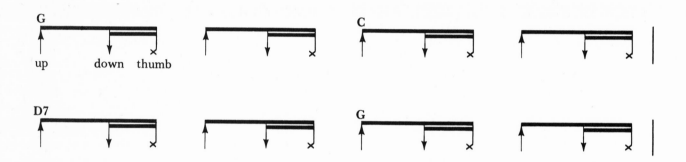

You may notice that the fifth string, which is tuned to the note G, harmonizes perfectly with the G and C chords but not with the D7. This effect—the unchanging note sounding through a number of different chords—is called a *drone*. The ear will accept a drone with only a limited number of chords, and this in turn limits the effective scope of the banjo (played in this manner) to certain types of songs. As you progress in your studies you will see why this is so, what types of songs sound best on the banjo, and, also, how to overcome this restriction.

Now we are ready to do some singin' and pickin' . . . .

Worried Man

takes a wor-ried man to sing a wor-ried song, It takes a wor-ried man to

sing a wor-ried song, I'm wor-ried now,_____ but I won't be wor-ried long.

G
I went across the river and I lay down to sleep,
C   G
I went across the river and I lay down to sleep,

I went across the river and I lay down to sleep,
      D7   G
When I woke up—had shackles on my feet. *Chorus*

G
Twenty-nine links of chain around my leg,
C   G
Twenty-nine links of chain around my leg,

Twenty-nine links of chain around my leg,
      D7   G
And on each link, an initial of my name. *Chorus*

G
I asked the judge, "What's gonna be my fine?"
C   G
I asked the judge, "What's gonna be my fine?"

I asked the judge, "What's gonna be my fine?"
      D7   G
"Twenty-one years on the Rocky Mountain Line."

Chorus

G
Twenty-one years to pay my awful crime,
C   G
Twenty-one years to pay my awful crime,

Twenty-one years to pay my awful crime,
      D7   G
Twenty-one years—but I got ninety-nine. *Chorus*

G
The train arrived, sixteen coaches long,
C   G
The train arrived, sixteen coaches long,

The train arrived, sixteen coaches long,
      D7   G
The girl I love is on that train and gone. *Chorus*

G
I looked down the track as far as I could see,
C   G
I looked down the track as far as I could see,

I looked down the track as far as I could see,
      D7   G
Little bitty hand was waving after me. *Chorus*

G
If anyone should ask you, who composed this song,
C   G
If anyone should ask you, who composed this song,

If anyone should ask you, who composed this song,
      D7   G
Tell him it was I, and I sing it all day long. *Chorus*

Little Brown Jug

My wife and I lived all a - lone in a

lit - tle log hut we called our home. She loved whis - ky, I loved rum, I

tell you what, We'd lots of fun. Ha, ha, ha, you and me, Lit - tle brown jug, don't

I love thee. Ha, ha, ha, you and me, lit - tle brown jug, don't I love thee.

       G   C
'Tis you that makes my friends my foes,
     D7   G
'Tis you that makes me wear old clothes;
              C
But here you are so near my nose,
    D7   G
So tip her up and down she goes. *Chorus*

           G   C
When I go toiling on my farm,
D7   G
Little brown jug beneath my arm;
             C
Set her near some shady tree—
D7   G
Little brown jug, don't I love thee? *Chorus*

G   C
I lay in the shade of a tree,
D7   G
Little brown jug in the shade of me.

             C
I raised her up and gave a pull—
D7   G
Little brown jug was about half full. *Chorus*

G   C
Crossed the creek on a hollow log,
D7   G
Me and the wife and the little brown dog.
             C
The wife and the dog fell into the bog,
    D7   G
But I held on to the little brown jug. *Chorus*

          G   C
One day when I went out to my farm,
D7   G
Little brown jug was under my arm,
             C
Stubbed my toe and down I fell—
D7   G
Broke that little jug all to hell. *Chorus*

G   C
When I die, don't bury me at all,
    D7   G
Just pickle my bones in alcohol.
             C
Put a bottle of booze at my head and feet,
    D7   G
And then I know that I will keep. *Chorus*

Old Dan Tucker

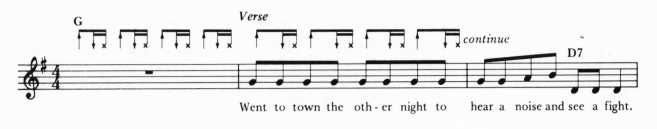

Went to town the oth-er night to hear a noise and see a fight.

All the peo-ple were stand-in' a-round, Say-in' Old Dan Tuck-er's come to town.

Chorus

Get out the way, Old Dan Tuck-er, You're too late to come for sup-per,

Sup-per's ov-er and din-ner's cook-in', And Old Dan Tuck-er's just stand-in' there look-in'.

G
Old Dan Tucker's a fine old man,

D7
Washed his face in a frying pan.

G
Combed his hair with a wagon wheel,

         D7   G
And died with a toothache in his heel. *Chorus*

G
Old Dan Tucker come to town,

D7
Riding a billygoat, leading a hound.

G
Hound barked and the billygoat jumped—

         D7   G
Throwed Old Dan right straddle of a stump. *Chorus*

G
Old Dan Tucker clumb a tree,

D7
His Lord and Master for to see.

G
The limb, it broke and Dan got a fall,

         D7   G
Never got to see his Lord at all. *Chorus*

G
Old Dan Tucker he got drunk,

D7
Fell in the fire and kicked up a chunk.

G
Red-hot coal got in his shoe,

         D7   G
Lord godamighty, how the ashes flew! *Chorus*

G
Old Dan Tucker come to town,

D7
Swinging the ladies 'round and 'round.

G
First to the right and then to the left,

         D7   G
And then to the one that you love best. *Chorus*

Pick a Bale of Cotton

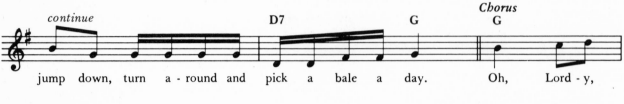

```
          G                C              G
Me and my wife can pick a bale of cotton,
                         D7            G
Me and my wife can pick a bale a day. Chorus

  G                  C                G
Me and my partner can pick a bale of cotton,
                          D7            G
Me and my partner can pick a bale a day. Chorus

       G                    C              G
I believe to my soul I can pick a bale of cotton,
                          D7             G
I believe to my soul I can pick a bale a day. Chorus

                G                   C            G
You got to do some picking to pick a bale of cotton,
                           D7             G
You got to do some picking to pick a bale a day. Chorus

            G                          C                 G
You got to pick a, pick a, pick a, pick a, pick a bale of cotton,
                                      D7            G
You got to pick a, pick a, pick a, pick a, pick a bale a day. Chorus
```

The C Tuning

This tuning is used for playing in the key of C as well as other keys derived from C (more on this later). To retune the banjo from the G tuning to the C, you just lower the fourth string from D to C. This is done by turning the appropriate tuning peg in the "loosening direction" until you have dropped one *whole tone.* Before you try anything, and if you are not quite sure what all this means, take a look at the following diagram of a C chord in the C tuning:

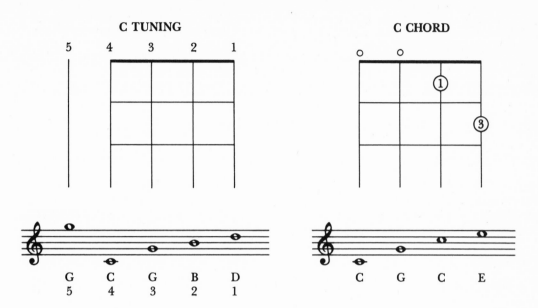

The note that the first finger is playing (on the second string) is C. Play it by itself.

It should sound an octave higher than the fourth string in the C tuning.

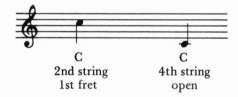

Now you have something to go by. Play that high C on the second string and sing that note to yourself. Keep that note in your mind and start loosening the fourth string slowly. *Keep playing the fourth string as you tune it* so that you can hear if you are getting there. Check back to the C on the second string. Tuning is a slow process of trial and error at first. When you think you've arrived play the C chord, string by string, slowly. How does it sound? Any adjustments necessary? (See page 148 for a more detailed analysis of tuning the banjo.)

In addition to the C chord, you'll need two more chords at present in the key of C:

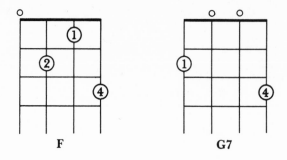

F   G7

Play the following songs using the basic banjo strum.

Oh, Susanna

I— come from Al - a - ba - ma with a
rained all night the day I left, the

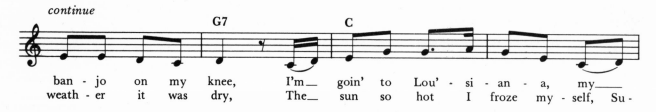

ban - jo on my knee, I'm— goin' to Lou' - si - an - a, my—
weath - er it was dry, The— sun so hot I froze my - self, Su -

true love for to see. It— Oh, Su - san - na, now
san - na, don't you cry.

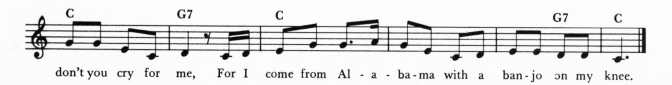

don't you cry for me, For I come from Al - a - ba - ma with a ban - jo on my knee.

     C
I had a dream the other night,

             G7
When everything was still.

     C
I thought I saw Susanna

        G7   C
A-coming down the hill.

The buckwheat cake was in her mouth,

             G7
The tear was in her eye.

      C
Says I, "I'm coming from the South."

     G7   C
Susanna, don't you cry. *Chorus*

Red River Valley

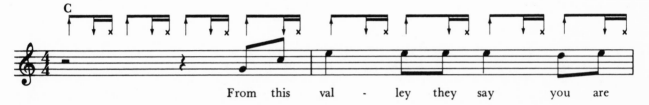

From this val - ley they say you are

continue

go - ing,___ We will miss your bright eyes and sweet smile. For they

say you are tak - ing the sun - shine_ That has bright-ened our path-way a - while.

<table>
<tr><td>

            C
Won't you think of the valley you're leaving?

          G7
Oh, how lonely and sad it will be.

   C   F
Oh, think of the fond heart you're breaking,

G7   C
And the grief you are causing me. *Chorus*

</td><td>

           C
From this valley they say you are going,

             G7
When you go, may your darling go, too?

    C   F
Would you leave her behind unprotected,

G7
When she loves no other but you? *Chorus*

</td></tr>
</table>

     C
I have promised you, darling, that never

               G7
Will a word from my lips cause you pain;

     C   F
And my life, it will be yours forever,

     G7   C
If you only will love me again. *Chorus*

It's Hard, Ain't It Hard

It's hard, and it's hard, ain't it

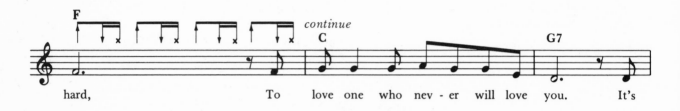

hard, To love one who nev-er will love you. It's

hard and it's hard, ain't it hard, great God, to love one who nev-er will be true.

C   F
There is a place in this old town,

 C   G7
And that's where my true love lays around.

 C   F
He takes other women down on his knee,

  C   G7   C
For to tell them what he never does tell me. *Chorus*

  C   F
Don't go there a-drinking and a-gambling,

  C   G7
Don't go your sorrows for to drown.

  C   F
That hard-likker place is a lowdown disgrace,

   C   G7   C
It's the meanest damn place in this town. *Chorus*

   C   F
The first time I saw my true love,

  C   G7
He was standing by the door.

  C   F
The last time I saw his false-hearted face

   C   G7   C
He was lying on the barroom floor. *Chorus*

Bury Me Beneath the Willow

Bur - y me be

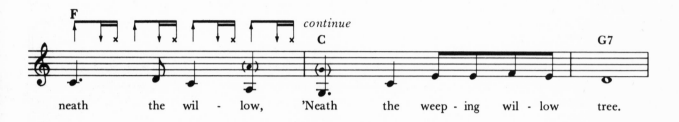

neath the wil - low, 'Neath the weep - ing wil - low tree.

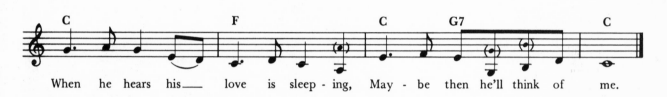

When he hears his____ love is sleep - ing, May - be then he'll think of me.

      C   F
My heart is sad and I am lonely,
C   G7
Thinking of the one I love.
C   F
When will I meet him? Oh, no never,
      C   G7   C
Unless we meet in heaven above. *Chorus*

      C   F
Tomorrow was to be our wedding,
 C   G7
I pray, oh Lord, where can he be?
       C   F
He's gone, he's gone to love another;
C   G7   C
He no longer cares for me. *Chorus*

      C   F
He told me that he dearly loved me,
C   G7
How could I believe him untrue?
      C   F
Until one day some neighbors told me,
 C   G7   C
"He has proven untrue to you." *Chorus*

PULLING-OFF AND HAMMERING-ON

There are occasions when notes are played on the banjo by the *left hand* alone. These notes are usually sandwiched in between the upstroke and the downstroke of the basic strum. Before we go into this new technique, retune your banjo back to the G tuning.

To do this you must reverse the process undertaken when you went from the G tuning to the C tuning; you must raise the pitch of the fourth string from its present note, C, to D. If you play the first string, you will hear what the note D should sound like (one octave higher than the desired note on the fourth string). Keep playing the fourth and first strings as you tighten the fourth. When you think you've arrived, play the open G chord. Does it sound right? If not, continue until the chord and the octave between strings one and four sound in tune.

One more thing . . . If you do not know how to read music it would be of great help if you began to work through the material dealing with note reading, beginning on page 144. As we go into matters of greater and greater complexity it will really become necessary for you to be able to make sense out of basic music notation. However, to make life easier at this point, we will use the following *tablature* (that is, a sort of non-music shorthand) to indicate where certain notes should be played: Under particular notes you will see two numbers, representing string and fret, respectively. The first number is the string, the second number is the fret:

> 4/2 = fourth string, second fret
> 3/0 = third string, open

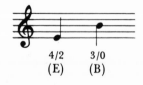

Pulling-off—G Tuning

Play the following note:

left hand

While the note, E, is still sounding—and without touching the string again with the right hand—flick or pull the third finger of your left hand sharply downward off the string. You should feel the finger catch momentarily against the string before it loses contact with it. That movement should cause the open string (D) to sound.

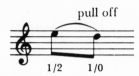

Don't rush the pull-off. Play E . . . let it sound . . . pull off . . .

In the basic strum the pull-off is played between the upstroke and the downstroke.

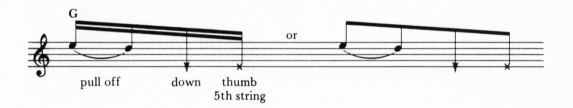

Again, don't rush. The four parts of the pull-off strum are all equal in terms of time (note value). Play them slowly and deliberately. Count out loud as you do it.

You don't have to pull off each time you play the strum. You may alternate a basic strum with a pull-off strum.

Try pulling off the same note while playing D7.

The Sow Got the Measles

How do you think I start-ed in life, I got me a sow and oth-er such things. Pig or hog or some such thing. The sow got the meas-les and she died in the spring.

G
What do you think I did with her hide?
D7   G
Made the best saddle you ever did ride.

Saddle or bridle or some such thing,
     D7
The sow got the measles

          G
     and she died in the spring.

G
What do you think I did with her tail?
D7   G
Made me a whip and also a flail.

Whip or whip-handle, some such thing,
     D7
The sow got the measles

          G ,
     and she died in the spring.

G
What do you think I did with her hair?
D7   G
Made the best satin you ever did wear.

Satin or silk or some such thing,
     D7
The sow got the measles

               G
     and she died in the spring.

G
What do you think I did with her feet?
D7   G
Made the best pickles you ever did eat.

Pickles or glue or some such thing,
     D7
The sow got the measles

               G
     and she died in the spring.

Green Corn

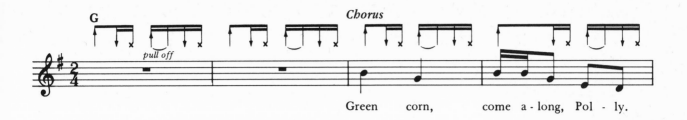

Green corn, come a-long, Pol-ly.

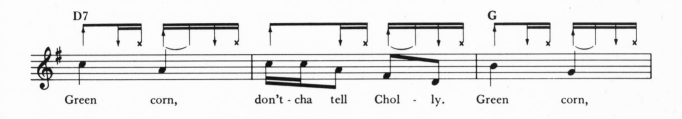

Green corn, don't-cha tell Chol-ly. Green corn,

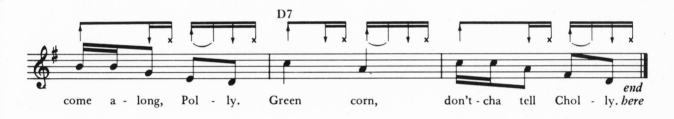

come a-long, Pol-ly. Green corn, don't-cha tell Chol-ly. *end here*

All I want in this cre-a-tion, Pret-ty lit-tle wife and a big plant-a-tion.

G
All I need to make me happy,

D7
Two little boys to call me pappy. *Chorus*

G
One named Bill, the other named Davey,

D7
They like their biscuits slopped in gravy. *Chorus*

G
All I need in this creation,

D7
Three month's work and nine vacation. *Chorus*

The pull-off for C sounds better this way:

left hand   2/3   2/1
                4   1

Jesse James

Jes - se James was a lad who —

killed man - y a man. He robbed the Glen - dale train. He — stole from the rich and he

gave to the poor, He'd a hand and a heart and a brain.

Poor Jes - se had a wife to mourn for her life, Three child - ren they were brave, But the

dirt - y lit - tle cow - ard who shot Mis - ter How - ard has laid poor — Jes - se in his grave.

          G   C   G
It was Robert Ford, that dirty little coward,
                  D7
I wonder how he does feel.
        G   C   G
For he ate of Jesse's bread and he slept in Jesse's bed,
              D7   G
And he laid poor Jesse in his grave. *Chorus*

<pre>
        G   C   G
How the people held their breath when they heard of Jesse's death,
                           D7
And wondered how he ever came to die.
         G   C   G
It was one of the gang, called Little Robert Ford
         D7   G
That shot poor Jesse on the sly. *Chorus*

G   C   G
Jesse was a man, a friend to the poor,
                           D7
He never would see a man suffer pain.
      G   C   G
And with his brother Frank he robbed the Chicago bank,
         D7   G
And stopped the Glendale train. *Chorus*

         G   C   G
It was on a Wednesday night, the moon was shining bright,
                     D7
They stopped the Glendale train.
         G   C   G
And the people, they did say for many miles away,
         D7   G
It was robbed by Frank and Jesse James. *Chorus*

         G   C   G
They went to a crossing not very far from there,
                  D7
And there they did the same.
         G   C   G
With the agent on his knees, he delivered up the keys
               D7   G
To the outlaws, Frank and Jesse James. *Chorus*

         G   C   G
It was on a Saturday night, Jesse was at home,
                  D7
Talking to his family brave.
         G   C   G
Robert Ford came along like a thief in the night
               D7   G
And laid poor Jesse in his grave. *Chorus*

         G   C   G
This song was made by Billy Gashade,
                     D7
As soon as the news did arrive.
      G   C   G
He said there was no man with the law in his hand
               D7   G
Who could take Jesse James while alive. *Chorus*
</pre>

The Boll Weevil

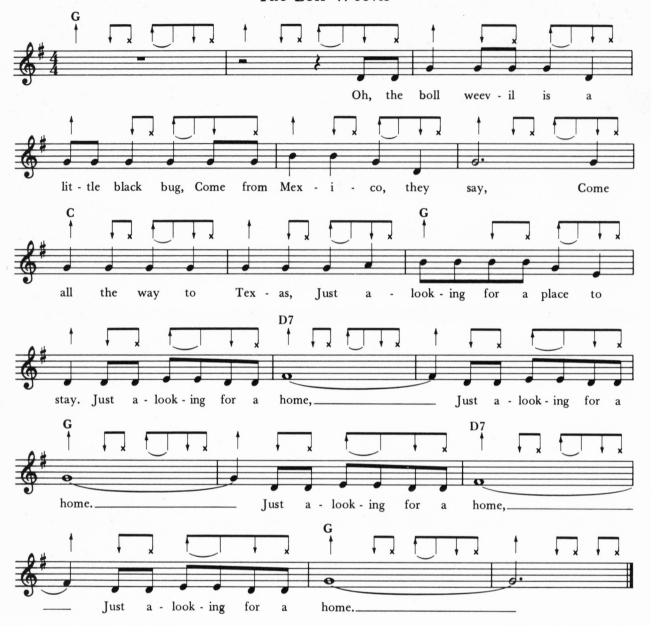

Oh, the boll weev - il is a lit - tle black bug, Come from Mex - i - co, they say, Come all the way to Tex - as, Just a - look - ing for a place to stay. Just a - look - ing for a home, _____ Just a - look - ing for a home. _____ Just a - look - ing for a home, _____ Just a - look - ing for a home. _____

G
The first time I seen the boll weevil,

He was sitting on the square.
C
The next time I saw the boll weevil,
G
He had all of his family there,
D7
Just a-looking for a home,
G
just a-looking for a home,
D7
Just a-looking for a home,
G
just a-looking for a home.

G
The farmer said to the weevil,

"What makes your face so red?"
C
The boll weevil said to the farmer,
G
"It's a wonder I ain't dead,
D7
Just a-looking for a home,
G
just a-looking for a home,
D7
Just a-looking for a home,
G
just a-looking for a home."

G
The farmer took the boll weevil,

And he put him in hot sand.
C
The boll weevil said, "This is mighty hot,
G
But I'll stand it like a man,
      D7   G
It'll be my home, it'll be my home,
      D7   G
It'll be my home, it'll be my home."

G
The farmer took the boll weevil,

And he put him in some ice.
C
The boll weevil said to the farmer,
G
"This is mighty cool and nice,
      D7   G
It'll be my home, it'll be my home,
      D7   G
It'll be my home, it'll be my home."

G
The boll weevil said to the farmer,

"You better leave me alone.
C
I ate up all your cotton
G
And I'm starting on your corn,
      D7   G
I'll have a home, I'll have a home,
      D7   G
I'll have a home, I'll have a home."

G
The farmer said to his wife,

"Now what do you think about that!
C
The boll weevil's gone and made a nest
G
In my brand-new Stetson hat,
      D7   G
And it's full of holes, it's full of holes,
      D7   G
It's full of holes, it's full of holes."

G
The farmer said to the merchant,

"We're in an awful fix.
C
The boll weevil ate all the cotton up,
G
And left us only sticks.
      D7   G
We've got no home, we've got no home,
      D7   G
We've got no home, we've got no home."

G
The farmer said to the merchant,

"We ain't made but one bale.
C
And before we give you that one,
G
We'll fight and go to jail.
      D7   G
We'll have a home, we'll have a home,
      D7   G
We'll have a home, we'll have a home."

G
And if anybody should ask you,

Who was it sang this song?
C
It was the poor old farmer
G
With all but his blue jeans gone,
      D7   G
A-looking for a home, a-looking for a home,
      D7   G
A-looking for a home, a-looking for a home.

Hammering-on—G Tuning

Another way to get a note to sound by the left hand alone is to strike the string sharply with a finger of the left hand. This is sort of the reverse process of pulling-off.

We begin by playing the open fourth string (D) in the usual manner, with the index finger of the right hand. While the string is still vibrating, hammer down on it with the second finger of the left hand at the second fret. You should hear the note E.

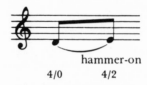

Again, as with the pull-off, don't rush. Play D . . . let it sound . . . hammer on.

After the hammer-on continue the basic strum. Don't rush. All four parts of the hammer-on strum are of equal note value. Play them slowly and deliberately. Count out loud as you do it.

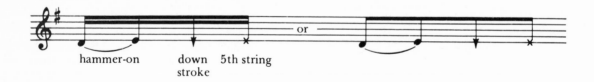

To hammer on a D7 chord you will have to change the fingering somewhat.

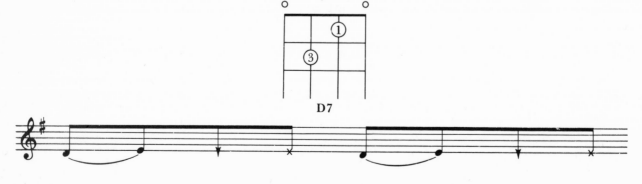

For C you may hammer either the fourth string, second fret,

or the first string, second fret:

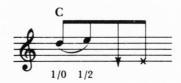

In actual practice the hammer-on strum is usually alternated with a basic strum.

Down by the Riverside

The symbol "¢" ("cut time") is often used in faster moving pieces. It tells you that each half note gets one beat. You therefore count each measure "1-2" rather than "1-2-3-4."

Gon-na lay down my sword and shield, down by the riv-er-side,— down by the riv-er-side,— down by the riv-er-side.— Gon-na lay down my sword and shield, down by the riv-er-side,— And stud-y war no more.— I ain't gon-na

Chorus

stud-y war no more, I ain't gon-na stud-y war no more, I ain't gon-na stud-y war no more,— I ain't gon-na more.— more.—

G
I'm gonna talk with the Prince of Peace,

    D7   G
Down by the riverside, down by the riverside, down by the riverside.

I'm gonna talk with the Prince of Peace,

                   D7   G
Down by the riverside, and study war no more. *Chorus*

      G
I'm gonna join hands with everyone,

                   D7   G
Down by the riverside, down by the riverside, down by the riverside.

Gonna join hands with everyone,

                   D7   G
Down by the riverside, and study war no more. *Chorus*

Roll in My Sweet Baby's Arms

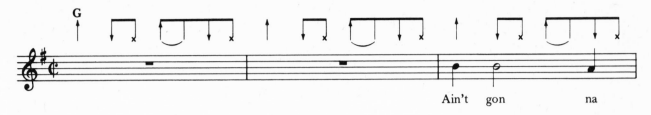

Ain't gon na

continue

live in the coun - try, _____ Ain't gon - na live on the

farm. ___ Well, I'll lay 'round the shack 'till the mail train comes

back, And I'll roll in my sweet ba - by's arms. _____

Chorus:
G
Roll in my sweet baby's arms,
           D7
Roll in my sweet baby's arms.
G   **C**
Lay 'round the shack 'til the mail train comes back,
    D7   **G**
Then I'll roll in my sweet baby's arms.

G
Sometimes there's a change in the ocean,
           D7
Sometimes there's a change in the sea.
   G   **C**
Sometimes there's a change in my own true love,
D7   **G**
But there's never a change in me. *Chorus*

G
Mama's a ginger-cake baker,
         D7
Sister can weave and spin.
G   **C**
Dad's got an interest in that old cotton mill,
    D7   **G**
Just watch that old money roll in. *Chorus*

         G
They tell me your parents don't like me—
               D7
They have drove me away from your door.
         G   **C**
If I had all my time to do over again,
       D7   **G**
I would never go there any more. *Chorus*

You don't have to stick to *all* hammering-on or *all* pulling-off throughout the entire accompaniment of any one song. Find your own variations and combinations.

The Wabash Cannonball

Rid - ing through the jun - gles on the Wa - bash Can - non - ball.

              G
Now, the eastern states are dandies,

              C
So the western people say.

   D7
From New York to St. Louis,

           G
And Chicago by the way.

Through the hills of Minnesota,

              C
Where the rippling waters fall,

  D7
No chances can be taken

           G
On the Wabash Cannonball. *Chorus*

G
Here's to Daddy Claxton,

           C
May his name forever stand.

D7
Will he be remembered

            G
Through parts of all our land.

When his earthly race is over

           C
And the curtain 'round him falls,

  D7
We'll bear him on to Victory

          G
On the Wabash Cannonball. *Chorus*

Pulling-off—C Tuning

Tune the fourth string down from D to C . . . .
Here are the pull-offs for C, G7 and F.

pull-off

3/2   3/0   3/2   3/0   2/3   2/1

The Big Rock Candy Mountain

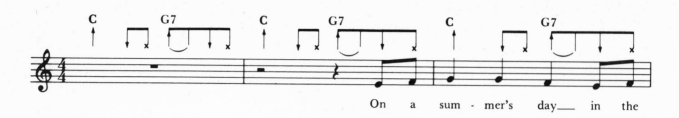

On a sum - mer's day— in the

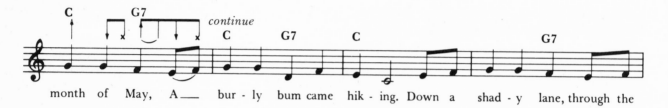

month of May, A— bur - ly bum came hik - ing. Down a shad - y lane, through the

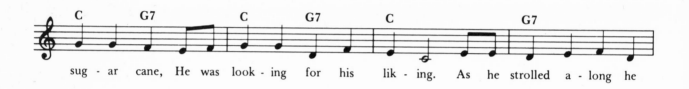

sug - ar cane, He was look - ing for his lik - ing. As he strolled a - long he

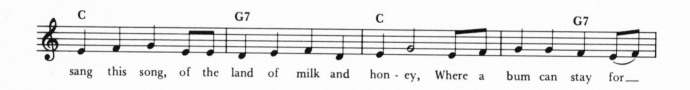

sang this song, of the land of milk and hon - ey, Where a bum can stay for—

man - y a day, And he won't need an - y mon - ey. Oh, the

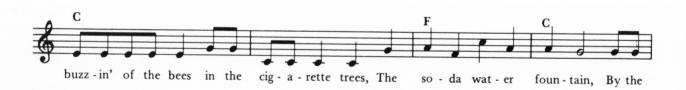

buzz - in' of the bees in the cig - a - rette trees, The so - da wat - er foun - tain, By the

lem - on - ade springs where the blue - bird sings, In the Big Rock Can - dy Moun - tain.

36

       C   G7   C   G7
In the Big Rock Candy Mountain, boys,
       C   G7   C
You never change your socks.
           G7   C   G7
And little streams of alkyhol
          C   G7   C
Come trickling down the rocks.
      G7   C
All the sheriffs have to tip their hats,
      G7   C
And the railroad bulls are blind.
             G7
There's a lake of stew,
    C   G7
And gingerale, too,
     C   G7   C
In the Big Rock Candy Mountain. *Chorus*

       C   G7   C   G7
In the Big Rock Candy Mountain, boys,
       C   G7   C
The cops have wooden legs.
          G7   C   G7
The bulldogs all have rubber teeth,
        C   G7   C
And the hens lay soft-boiled eggs.
    G7   C
The boxcars are all empty there,
      G7   C
And the sun shines every day.
          G7
I'm bound to go
          C   G7
Where there ain't no snow,
     C   G7   C
In the Big Rock Candy Mountain. *Chorus*

       C   G7   C   G7
In the Big Rock Candy Mountain, boys,
       C   G7   C
The jails are made of tin.
          G7   C   G7
And you can slip right out again,
     C   G7   C
Soon as they put you in.
    G7   C
There ain't no short-handled shovels there,
   G7   C
No axes, saws nor picks.
           G7
I'm bound to stay
        C   G7
Where they sleep all day,
     C   G7   C
In the Big Rock Candy Mountain. *Chorus*

The Banks of the Ohio

me,____ To take a walk____ a lit-tle way,____ And as we walked____ we had a

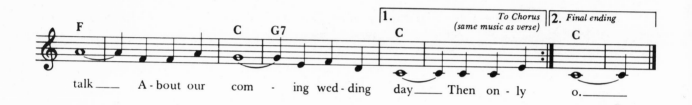

talk ____ A-bout our com - ing wed-ding day____ Then on-ly o.____

Chorus:
           C-G7   C
Then only say that you'll be mine,

           G7   C
And in no other arms entwine,

                  F
Down beside where the waters flow,

           C-G7   C
Along the banks of the Ohio.

       C-G7   C
I asked your mother for you, dear,
       G7   C
And she said you were too young.

             F
Only say that you'll be mine—
      C-G7   C
Happiness we then will find. *Chorus*

       C-G7   C
I held a knife against her breast,
       G7   C
As gently in my arms she pressed,

                     F
Crying, "Willie, oh Willie, don't murder me,
      C-G7   C
I'm unprepared for eternity." *Chorus*

       C-G7   C
I took her by her lily-white hand,
       G7   C
Led her down where the waters stand.

                  F
I picked her up and pitched her in,
      C-G7   C
For I knew she could not swim. *Chorus*

         C-G7   C
I started back home 'twixt twelve and one,
         G7   C
Crying, "My God, what have I done?

                  F
The woman I love has lost her life.
        C-G7   C
Because she would not be my wife." *Chorus*

Rise and Shine

Rise____ and shine____ and

continue

give God the glo - ry, glo - ry. Rise_ and shine_ and give God the glo - ry, glo - ry,

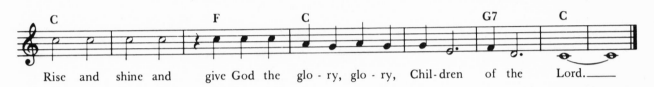

Rise and shine and give God the glo - ry, glo - ry, Chil-dren of the Lord.____

C
The Lord said, "Noah, there's gonna be a floody, floody."
G7
The Lord said, "Noah, there's gonna be a floody, floody,
C   F   C
Get your children out of the muddy, muddy!"
        G7   C
    Children of the Lord.

C
Noah, he built him, he built him an arky, arky,
G7
Noah, he built him, he built him an arky, arky.
C   F   C
Made it out of hickory barky, barky.
        G7   C
    Children of the Lord.

    C
The animals, they came, they came by twosy, twosy,
    G7
The animals, they came, they came by twosy, twosy.
C   F   C
Elephants and kangaroosy, roosy.
        G7   C
    Children of the Lord.

    C
The sun came out and dried up the landy, landy,
    G7
The sun came out and dried up the landy, landy.
C   F   C
Everything was fine and dandy, dandy.
        G7   C
    Children of the Lord. *Repeat verse one.*

Hammering-on—C Tuning

Oleana

Oh, to be in O - le - an - a,

That's where I'd like to be, Than be bound in Nor - way and drag the chains of slav - er - y.

Chorus

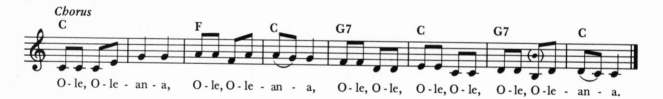

O - le, O - le - an - a, O - le, O - le - an - a, O - le, O - le, O - le, O - le, O - le, O - le - an - a.

C
In Oleana land is free,

F   C
The wheat and corn just plant themselves,

  G7   C
Then grow a good four feet a day,

  G7   C
While on your bed you rest yourself. *Chorus*

C
Beer as sweet as Munchener

F   C
Springs from the ground and flows away.

  G7   C
The cows all like to milk themselves,

  G7   C
And the hens lay eggs ten times a day. *Chorus*

C
Little roasted piggies there

F   C
Rush about the city streets,

  G7   C
Inquiring so politely

  G7   C
If a slice of ham you'd like to eat. *Chorus*

C
Say, if you'd begin to live,

        F   C
To Oleana you must go;

  G7   C
The poorest wretch in Norway

  G7   C
Becomes a duke in a year or so. *Chorus*

East Virginia

I was born _____ in East Vir-

continue

gin - ia, _____ North Car - o - li - na I did go. ____ There I met__

__ a fair young maid - en, _____ And whose name__ I did__ not know. __

            C
Well, her hair was dark of color,
       F   C
Cheeks they were a rosy red.
     F   C
On her breast she wore white lilies—
      G7   C
Where I longed to lay my head.

           C
I'd rather live in some dark holler,
       F   C
Where the sun would never shine,
      F   C
Than for you to love another,
      G7   C
And to know you'd never be mine.

           C
I don't want your greenback dollar,
      F   C
I don't want your silver chain,
      F   C
All I want is your love, darling:
      G7   C
Say that you'll be mine again.

Camptown Races

Verse

Camp - town la - dies sing this song, doo dah, doo dah, Camp - town race - track five miles long, Oh, doo dah day. Go down there with my hat caved in, doo dah, doo dah, Come back home with my pock - et full of tin,

Chorus

Oh, doo dah day. Goin' to run all night, Goin' to run all day. Bet my mon - ey on the bob - tail nag, Some - bod - y bet on the bay.

       C
The long-tail filly and the big black hoss,
       G7
       Doo-dah, doo-dah,
      C
They fly the track and they both cut across,
       G7   C
       Oh, doo-dah day.

The blind hoss stickin' in a big mud hole,
       G7
       Doo-dah, doo-dah,
    C
Can't touch bottom with a ten-foot pole,
       G7   C
       Oh, doo-dah day. *Chorus*

       C
Old muley cow come onto the track,
       G7
     Doo-dah, doo-dah,
       C
The bobtail fling her over his back,
     G7   C
     Oh, doo-dah day.

Then fly along like a railroad car,
       G7
     Doo-dah, doo-dah,
C
Running a race with a shooting star,
     G7   C
     Oh, doo-dah day. *Chorus*

     C
See them flying on a ten-mile heat,
       G7
     Doo-dah, doo-dah,
     C
'Round the race track, then repeat,
     G7   C
     Oh, doo-dah day.

I win my money on the bobtail nag,
       G7
     Doo-dah, doo-dah,
      C
I keep my money in an old towbag,
     G7   C
     Oh, doo-dah day. *Chorus*

CHAPTER THREE

TRANSPOSING

Too High? Too Low?

You may have noticed that some of the songs we have learned so far were either too high or too low for your voice. If that has been the case, don't worry, there's nothing wrong with you. Some people have high vocal ranges, others have lower ranges. You must learn how to adapt any song to *your* own range. This adaptation is called *transposing*.

The process of transposing (or transposition) is derived from the basic fact that a melody may begin on any note. Once that starting note has been established all the other notes (and chords) are pre-determined. The *relationship* between the notes and the chords is what we transpose from one key to another.

For example, if we have a song in the key of C whose chords are C, F and G7 and we wish to transpose it to another key, we must first determine the relationship between those three chords. This is done as follows. The scale of C major is made up of the notes

From this we see that C is the first note, F is the fourth and G is the fifth. It is this relationship (I, IV, V—Roman numbers are used when referring to chords) that we transpose to the new key by figuring out the I, IV and V of that new key. We merely substitute the first note of the desired key for I and the other chords fall into place. The numerical relationship between the chords is maintained. To illustrate this clearly here is a table of I, IV and V7 chords in five commonly played keys. (We add the "7" to the V. The transposition is not affected by this.)

Key	*I*	*IV*	*V7*
C	C	F	G7
G	G	C	D7
D	D	G	A7
A	A	D	E7
E	E	A	B7

From this table you can proceed in either of two directions, depending on what the problem is.

If you come across a song whose I, IV and V7 chords are unfamiliar to you, you may transpose them directly to C or G. The choice, C or G, depends entirely on your vocal range. It is not correct to say that you sing best in C (or G). You will have to try each song you come across to decide upon the key.

The Capo

The other possibility is to learn to play in the new, unfamiliar key. This is usually done with the aid of a *capo*.

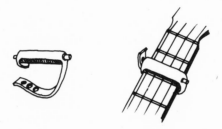

The capo is a small elastic clamp that fits over the neck of the banjo and presses down uniformly over strings 1, 2, 3 and 4. It may be placed at any fret and will raise the pitch of the four strings *one half-step* for each fret. The fifth string must also be retuned so that it is always an octave higher than the third. (More on this in a minute.)

Now, if you see a song whose chords are D, G and A7 you place the capo on the second fret and play (above the capo) C, F and G7. The capo has transposed you from C to D. You think and finger in C but the banjo is in D.

If you see a song whose chords are A, D and E7, you place the capo on the second fret and play G, C and D7. The capo has transposed you from G to A. You think and finger in G but the banjo is in A.

"But," I hear you say, "how do I know which banjo tuning to use for other keys, where do I put the capo and what if there are more than three chords?"

Good questions. Let's deal with the first two first, namely: which tuning to use for other keys and where to put the capo.

G Tuning

Key	Capo on fret	I	IV	V7
G	0	G	C	D7
A♭	1	A♭	D♭	E♭7
A	2	A	D	E7
B♭	3	B♭	E♭	F7
B	4	B	E	F♯7

C Tuning

Key	Capo on fret	I	IV	V7
C	0	C	F	G7
Db(C♯)	1	Db(C♯)	Gb(F♯)	Ab7(G♯7)
D	2	D	G	A7
Eb	3	Eb	Ab	Bb7
E	4	E	A	B7
F	5	F	Bb	C7
Gb(F♯)	6	Gb(F♯)	Cb(B)	Db7(C♯7)

To get the capo properly positioned on the fifth fret for F you will have to lay it diagonally against the fifth string tuning peg. It may not always be possible to get a clear tone on the open strings because of this awkward placement.

To get the capo properly positioned on the sixth fret for Gb(F♯) you will have to remove it and replace it above the fifth fret tuning peg. This, too, is not too convenient—but it can be done if need be.

There is another way to get these (and other) awkward keys. See page 149 for an interesting solution.

Retuning the Fifth String as the Capo Moves Upward

The fifth string must always be one octave higher than the third string. (It is also the same note as the fifth fret of the first string. Remember, the fifth fret "rises" as the capo rises.)

It is possible to tune the fifth string up one or two notes to accommodate the capo on the first and second frets. To tighten it any more as the capo goes to the third fret and beyond, is to run the risk of breaking the string. To overcome this difficulty most banjos should be equipped with a little hook or screw just before the fifth fret above the fifth string peg which serves as an auxiliary "capo" for the fifth string. You merely slip the fifth string under this hook and tune to the required note.

Before   After

See if you can put all this together by trying some of the songs we have already done in different keys—perhaps in keys that better suit your own vocal range. Then we'll go on.

Using the Capo to Transpose

We now come to the practical application of the theoretical information just explained. To play the following songs you will have to move the capo to the proper fret and retune the fifth string (not forgetting the correct tuning for the banjo).

As an aid for those of you who would care to read the music, the tunes have been written out in two keys—the actual key as determined by the capo, and C or G (depending on the tuning). The note readers will do their thing in C or G. The chords have been written out in C or G for reference purposes in addition to the actual chords in the capo-derived key. In a very short time, hopefully, you will not need to refer to these C/G chords but will just be able to transpose quickly into the new keys. The next, and final, stage is to *hear* the correct chord changes without having to refer to the printed page at all.

Use the basic banjo strum and embellish with hammering-on and pulling-off throughout.

Go Tell Aunt Rhody

C tuning

capo 2

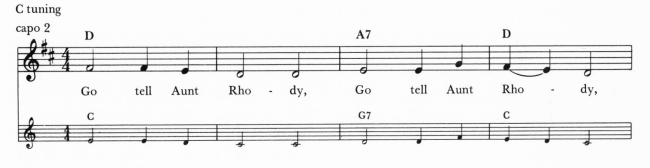

Go tell Aunt Rho - dy, Go tell Aunt Rho - dy,

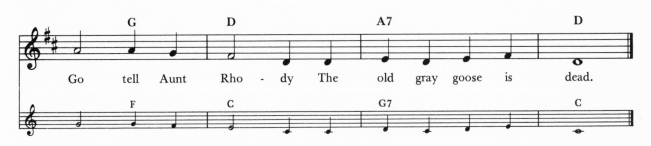

Go tell Aunt Rho - dy The old gray goose is dead.

D
The one that she's been saving,
A7 D
The one that she's been saving,
  G D
The one that she's been saving,
A7 D
To make her featherbed.

D
The goslings are crying,
A7 D
The goslings are crying,
  G D
The goslings are crying,
A7   D
Because their mama's dead.

D
She died in the mill pond,
A7 D
She died in the mill pond,
  G D
She died in the mill pond,
A7   D
A-standing on her head.

Going Down the Road Feeling Bad

C tuning
capo 4

I'm go-ing down the road feel-ing bad, I'm__ go-ing down the road feel-ing bad, I'm go-ing down the road feel-ing bad, Lord, Lord__ And I ain't gon-na be treat-ed this-a - way.

E
I'm going where the climate suits my clothes,

A   E
I'm going where the climate suits my clothes,

A   E
I'm going where the climate suits my clothes, Lord, Lord,

B7   E
And I ain't gonna be treated thisaway.

E
Two-dollar shoes hurt my feet,

A   E
Two-dollar shoes hurt my feet,

A   E
Two-dollar shoes hurt my feet, Lord, Lord,

B7   E
And I ain't gonna be treated thisaway.

E
Ten-dollar shoes suit me fine,

A   E
Ten-dollar shoes suit me fine,

A   E
Ten-dollar shoes suit me fine, Lord, Lord,

B7   E
And I ain't gonna be treated thisaway.

E
I'm down in the jailhouse on my knees,

A   E
I'm down in the jailhouse on my knees,

A   E
I'm down in the jailhouse on my knees, Lord, Lord,

B7   E
And I ain't gonna be treated thisaway.

E
I'm going where the water tastes like wine,
A   E
I'm going where the water tastes like wine,
A   E
I'm going where the water tastes like wine, Lord, Lord,
B7   E
'Cause this prison water tastes like turpentine.

Jacob's Ladder

A
Every rung goes higher and higher,
E7   A
Every rung goes higher and higher,
            D   A
Every rung goes higher and higher,
    E7   A
Children of the Lord.

A
Every new man makes us stronger,
E7   A
Every new man makes us stronger,
                D   A
Every new man makes us stronger,
        E7   A
Children of the Lord.

            A
We have toiled in dark and danger,
E7   A
We have toiled in dark and danger,
            D   A
We have toiled in dark and danger,
        E7   A
Children of the Lord. *Repeat verse one*

Oh, Mary, Don't You Weep

C tuning
capo 5

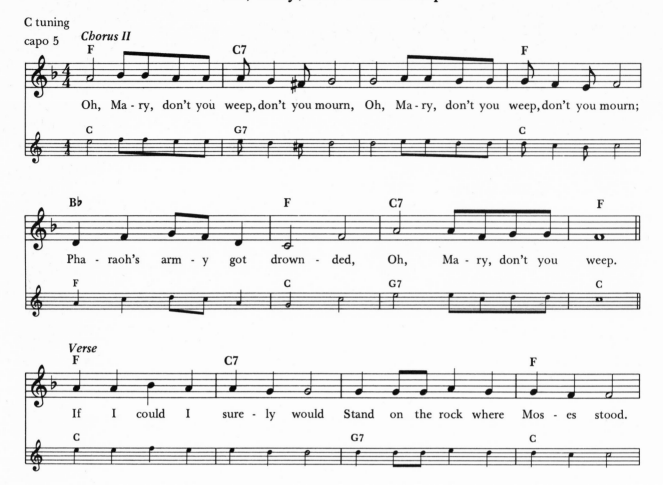

Oh, Mary, don't you weep, don't you mourn, Oh, Mary, don't you weep, don't you mourn;

Pharaoh's arm-y got drown-ded, Oh, Mary, don't you weep.

Verse

If I could I sure-ly would Stand on the rock where Mos-es stood.

Chorus I

Pharaoh's arm-y got drown-ded, Oh, Mary don't you weep.

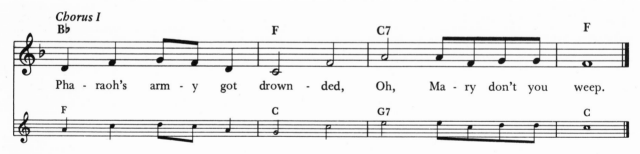

F   C7
Moses stood on the Red Sea shore,
          F
Smitin' that water with a two-by-four.

    Chorus I & II

F   C7
One of these nights about twelve o'clock,
         F
This old world's gonna reel and rock.

    Chorus I & II

F   C7
God gave Noah the rainbow sign,
          F
"No more water, but fire next time!"

    Chorus I & II

F   C7
I may be right and I may be wrong,
            F
I know you're gonna miss me when I'm gone.

    Chorus I & II

Buffalo Gals

G tuning
capo 3

Verse

As I was walk-ing down the street, down the street, down the street, A pret-ty girl I chanced to meet, And she was fair to see.

Chorus

Buf-fa-lo gals, won't you come out to-night, Won't you come out to-night, Won't you come out to-night?

Buf-fa-lo gals, won't you come out to-night, And dance by the light of the moon.

Bb
Oh, yes pretty boys, we're coming out tonight,
F7 **Bb**
Coming out tonight, coming out tonight.

Oh, yes pretty boys, we're coming out tonight,
F7 **Bb**
To dance by the light of the moon. *Chorus*

Bb
I danced with a gal with a hole in her stocking,
F7 **Bb**
And her heel kept a-rocking and her toe kept a-knocking.

I danced with a gal with a hole in her stocking,
F7 **Bb**
And we danced by the light of the moon. *Chorus*

CHAPTER FOUR

THREE-QUARTER ($\frac{3}{4}$) TIME

Up to now the essential metrical feeling of the songs and the strum has been either "one-two . . . one-two . . ." ($\frac{2}{4}$) or "one-two-three-four . . ." ($\frac{4}{4}$). Many songs, however, have the feeling of "one-two-three . . . one-two-three." Sometimes this is called "waltz time"—although not every song with the "one-two-three" beat is necessarily a waltz. More properly this metrical arrangement is referred to as *three-quarter time*. Its indication in the music proper is the symbol "$\frac{3}{4}$" at the beginning of the piece.

The Basic Banjo $\frac{3}{4}$ Strum

Just add another downstroke and thumb beat to the original basic strum.

On Top of Old Smoky

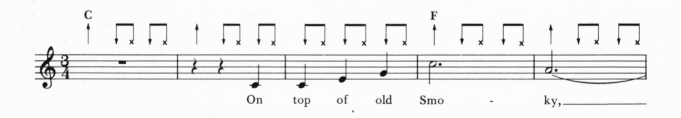

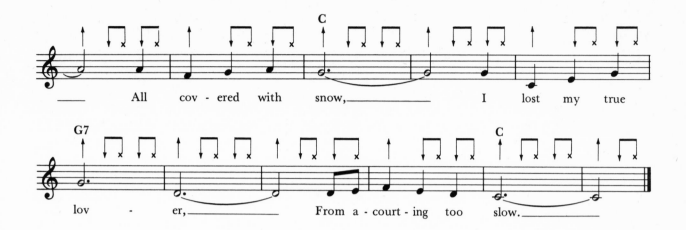

All cov-ered with snow, _____ I lost my true lov - er, _____ From a - court - ing too slow. _____

C   F
A-courting's a pleasure,
C
And parting is grief.
            G7
But a false-hearted lover
      C
Is worse than a thief.

C   F
A thief, he will rob you,
         C
And take what you have,
            G7
But a false-hearted lover
          C
Will send you to your grave.

       C   F
The grave will decay you,
        C
And turn you to dust.
           G7
And where is the young man
       C
A poor girl can trust.

          C   F
They'll hug you and kiss you,
            C
And tell you more lies,
                  G7
Than the cross-ties on the railroad
            C
Or the stars in the skies.

          C   F
They'll tell you they love you,
            C
Just to give your heart ease.
              G7
But the minute your back's turned,
             C
They'll court whom they please.

          C   F
So, come all you young maidens
           C
And listen to me.
            G7
Never place your affection
           C
On a green willow tree.

         C   F
For the leaves, they will wither,
           C
And the roots, they will die,
              G7
And your true love will leave you,
           C
And you'll never know why.

Hard Is the Fortune of All Womankind

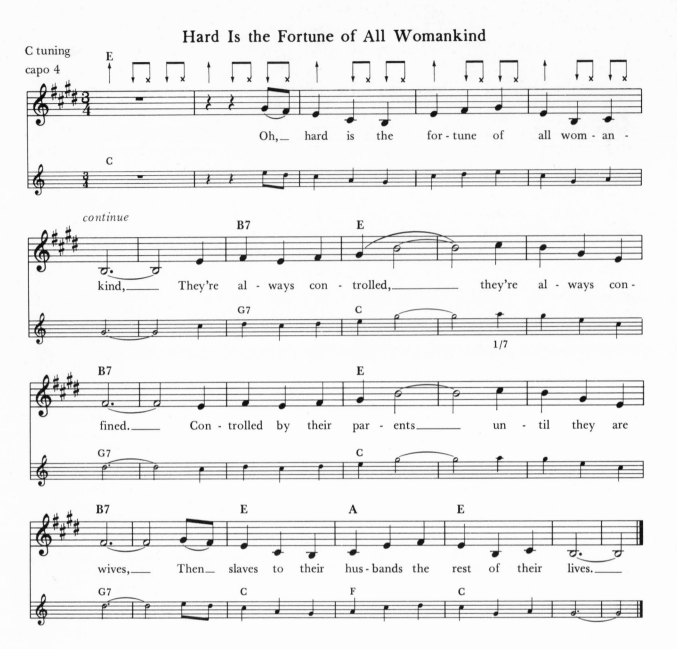

Oh, I am a poor girl, my fortune is sad,
I have always been courted by the wagoner's lad.
He courted me daily, by night and by day,
And now he is loaded and going away.

Your horses are hungry, go feed them some hay,
Come sit down beside me as long as you may.
My horses ain't hungry, they won't eat your hay,
So, fare you well, darling, I'll be on my way.

Your parents don't like me because I am poor.
They say I'm not worthy of entering your door.
I work for my living, my money's my own,
And if they don't like me they can leave me alone.

Your wagon needs greasing, your whip is to mend,
Come sit down here by me as long as you can.
My wagon is greasy, my whip's in my hand,
So, fare you well, darling, no longer to stand.

54

My Bonny Lies Over the Ocean

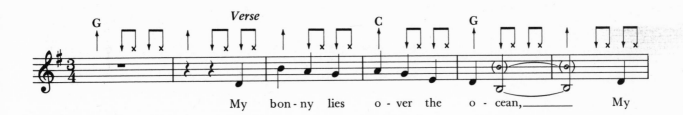

My bon-ny lies o-ver the o-cean,_____ My

Lay the 1st finger across all the strings at fret 2.

continue

bon-ny lies o-ver the sea,_____ My bon-ny lies o-ver the o-cean,_____ Please

Chorus

bring back my bon-ny to me._____ Bring back, bring back, Oh, bring back my

bon-ny to me, to me. Bring back, bring back, Oh, bring back my bon-ny to me._____

G   C   G
Oh, blow, ye winds over the ocean,
           A(7)   D7
And blow, ye winds over the sea.
   G   C   G
Oh, blow, ye winds over the ocean,
   C   D7   G
And bring back my bonny to me. *Chorus*

G   C   G
Last night as I lay on my pillow,
         A(7)   D7
Last night as I lay on my bed.
   G   C   G
Last night as I lay on my pillow,
   C   D7   G
I dreamed that my bonny was dead. *Chorus*

           G   C   G
The winds have blown over the ocean,
           G   A(7)   D7
The winds have blown over the sea.
           G   C   G
The winds have blown over the ocean,
           C   D7   G
And brought back my bonny to me. *Chorus*

Blow the Man Down

C tuning
capo 2

As I was a - walk - ing down Par - a - dise Street, To me way, aye, blow the man down, A pret - ty young dam - sel I chanced for to meet, Give me some time to blow the man down.

                            D
Chorus: Oh, blow the man down, bullies, blow the man down,

                                    A7
               To me way, aye, blow the man down,

Oh, blow the man down, bullies, blow him right down,

                                D
          Give me some time to blow the man down.

        D
She was round in the counter and bluff in the bow,

        A7
    To me way, aye, blow the man down,

So I took in all sail and cried, "Way enough now!"

              D
    Give me some time to blow the man down. *Chorus*

     D
I hailed her in English, she answered me clear,

        A7
    To me way, aye, blow the man down,

"I'm from the 'Black Arrow' bound to the 'Shakespeare',"

             D
    Give me some time to blow the man down. *Chorus*

D
So I tailed her my flipper and took her in tow,
         A7
    To me way, aye, blow the man down,

And yardarm to yardarm away we did go,
                        D
    Give me some time to blow the man down. *Chorus*

        D
And as we were going she said unto me,
         A7
    To me way, aye, blow the man down,

"There's a spanking full-rigger just ready for sea."
                    D
    Give me some time to blow the man down. *Chorus*

        D
That spanking full-rigger for New York was bound,
         A7
    To me way, aye, blow the man down,

She was very well manned and very well found,
                    D
    Give me some time to blow the man down. *Chorus*

          D
But as soon as that packet was clear of the bar,
         A7
    To me way, aye, blow the man down,

The mate knocked me down with the end of a spar,
                    D
    Give me some time to blow the man down. *Chorus*

          D
And as soon as that packet was out on the sea,
         A7
    To me way, aye, blow the man down,

'Twas devlish hard treatment of every degree,
                    D
    Give me some time to blow the man down. *Chorus*

       D
So, I give you fair warning before we belay,
         A7
    To me way, aye, blow the man down,

Don't never take heed of what pretty girls say,
                    D
    Give me some time to blow the man down. *Chorus*

Who's Gonna Shoe Your Pretty Little Foot?

G tuning
capo 2

Who's gon-na shoe your pret-ty lit-tle foot?

Who's gon-na glove your hand?

Who's gon-na kiss your red ru-by lips?

Who's gon-na be your man?

A
Who's gonna be your man?
D   A
Who's gonna be your man?
D   A
Who's gonna kiss your red ruby lips?
E7   A
Who's gonna be your man?

A
Papa's gonna shoe my pretty little foot,

D   A
Mama's gonna glove my hand.

D   A
Sister's gonna kiss my red ruby lips,

E7   A
I don't need no man.

A
I don't need no man,

D   A
I don't need no man.

D   A
Sister's gonna kiss my red ruby lips,

E7   A
I don't need no man.

        A
The longest train I ever did see

    D   A
Was a hundred coaches long.

    D   A
The only woman I ever did love

    E7   A
Was on that train and gone.

A
On that train and gone,

D   A
On that train and gone,

    D   A
The only woman I ever did love

    E7   A
Was on that train and gone.

Hammering-on and Pulling-off In ¾ Time

Since the hammer-on and the pull-off take place on the first beat (up-stroke) of the strum they are not affected by metrical changes from 4/4 to 3/4.

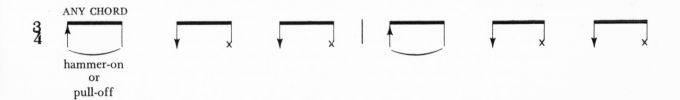

Embellish the following songs (and the preceding ones as well) with hammering-on and pulling-off as you like it.

Abdullah Bulbul Amir

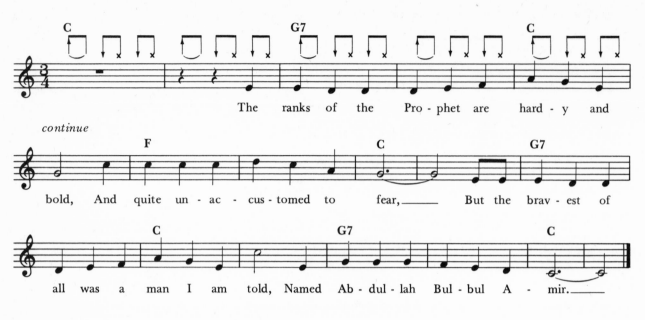

The ranks of the Pro-phet are hard-y and bold, And quite un-ac-cus-tomed to fear,____ But the brav-est of all was a man I am told, Named Ab-dul-lah Bul-bul A - mir.____

C   G7   C
When they needed a man to encourage the van,
    F   C
Or to harass the foe from the rear,
    G7   C
Storm fort or redoubt, they had only to shout
        G7   C
    For Abdullah Bulbul Amir.

C   G7   C
Now, the heroes were plenty and well known to fame,
    F   C
Who fought in the ranks of the Czar.
    G7   C
But the bravest of these was a man by the name
        G7   C
    Of Ivan Skavinsky Skivar.

C   G7   C
He could imitate Pushkin, play poker and pool,
    F   C
And strum on the Spanish guitar.
    G7   C
In fact, quite the cream of the Muscovite team,
        G7   C
    Was Ivan Skavinsky Skivar.

C   G7   C
One day this bold Russian had shouldered his gun,
    F   C
And donned his most truculent sneer,
    G7   C
Downtown he did go, where he trod on the toe
        G7   C
    Of Abdullah Bulbul Amir.

  C   G7   C
"Young man," quoth Bulbul, "has your life grown so dull
                          F   C
That you're anxious to end your career?
    G7   C
Vile infidel, know, you have trod on the toe
        G7   C
    Of Abdullah Bulbul Amir."

  C   G7   C
Said Ivan, "My friend, your remarks in the end
           F   C
Will avail you but little, I fear;
        G7   C
For you ne'er will survive to repeat them alive,
        G7   C
    Mister Abdullah Bulbul Amir."

  C   G7   C
They fought all that night 'neath the yellow moonlight,
         F   C
The din, it was heard from afar.
        G7   C
And huge multitudes came, so great was the fame
        G7   C
    Of Abdul and Ivan Skivar.

  C   G7   C
As Abdul's long knife was extracting the life,
        F   C
In fact, he had shouted, "Huzzah!"
        G7   C
He felt himself struck by that wily Calmuck,
            G7   C
    Count Ivan Skavinsky Skivar.

  C   G7   C
There's a tomb rises up where the Blue Danube rolls,
         F   C
And 'graved there in characters clear,
        G7   C
Is, "Stranger, when passing, oh, pray for the soul
        G7   C
    Of Abdullah Bulbul Amir."

  C   G7   C
A Muscovite maiden, her lone vigil keeps,
         F   C
'Neath the light of the pale polar star.
        G7   C
And the name that she murmurs so oft as she weeps,
        G7   C
    Is Ivan Skavinsky Skivar.

The Devil and the Farmer's Wife

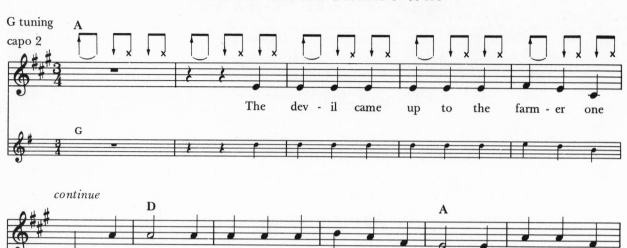

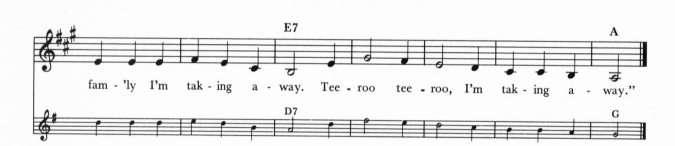

         A
"Oh, please don't take my eldest son,

         D   A
    Teeroo, teeroo, my eldest son,

                              E7
There's work on the farm that's got to be done,

                       A
    Teeroo, teeroo, that's got to be done."

           A
"Take my wife, take my wife, with the joy of my heart,

         D   A
    Teeroo, teeroo, with the joy of my heart,

                          E7
And I hope, by golly, that you never part,

                      A
    Teeroo, teeroo, that you never part."

         A
The Devil put the old lady into a sack,

         D   A
    Teeroo, teeroo, into a sack.

                       E7
And down the road he goes clickety-clack,

                   A
    Teeroo, teeroo, he goes clickety-clack.

          A
When the Devil got her to the gates of hell,
      D   A
   Teeroo, teeroo, to the gates of hell,
                            E7
He says, "Poke up the fires, we'll bake her well,
                       A
   Teeroo, teeroo, we'll bake her well."

      A
Up came a little devil with a ball and chain,
      D   A
   Teeroo, teeroo, with a ball and chain,
                        E7
She upped with her foot and she kicked out his brains,
                    A
   Teeroo, teeroo, she kicked out his brains.

      A
Then nine little devils went climbing the wall,
      D   A
   Teeroo, teeroo, went climbing the wall,
                        E7
Screaming, "Take her back, Daddy, she'll murder us all,
                    A
   Teeroo, teeroo, she'll murder us all."

      A
The old man was peeping out of the crack,
      D   A
   Teeroo, teeroo, out of the crack,
                        E7
When he saw the old Devil come bringing her back,
                  A
   Teeroo, teeroo, come bringing her back.

      A
He says, "Here's your wife, both sound and well,
      D   A
   Teeroo, teeroo, both sound and well,
                        E7
If I kept her there longer she'd have torn up hell,
                  A
   Teeroo, teeroo, she'd have torn up hell."

        A
He says, "I've been a devil 'most all of my life,
      D   A
   Teeroo, teeroo, 'most all of my life,
                      E7
But I ain't been in hell till I met with your wife.
                  A
   Teeroo, teeroo, till I met with your wife."

      A
This proves that the women are better than men,
      D   A
   Teeroo, teeroo, are better than men,
                    E7
They can all go to hell and come back again,
                 A
   Teeroo, teeroo, and come back again.

Rye Whisky

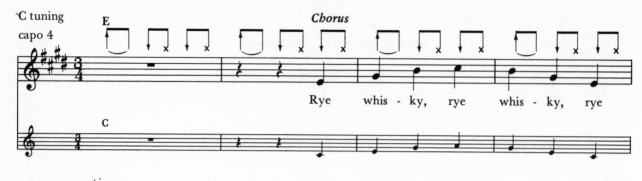

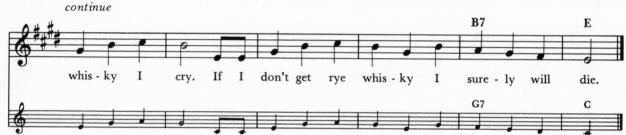

       E
I'll eat when I'm hungry, I'll drink when I'm dry,

                         B7   E
If the hard times don't kill me, I'll live till I die. *Chorus*

   E
Beefsteak when I'm hungry, red likker when I'm dry,

                     B7   E
Greenbacks when I'm hard up and religion when I die. *Chorus*

       E
If the ocean was whisky and I was a duck,

              B7   E
I'd dive to the bottom for just one sweet suck. *Chorus*

       E
But the ocean ain't whisky and I ain't a duck,

               B7   E
So I'll play jack-o-diamonds and trust to my luck. *Chorus*

       E
Jack-o-diamonds, jack-o-diamonds, I know you of old,

              B7   E
You robbed my poor pockets of silver and gold. *Chorus*

      E
Oh, whisky, you villain, you're no friend to me,

             B7   E
You killed my poor daddy, gol darn you, try me. *Chorus*

       E
You may boast of your knowledge and brag of your sense,

      B7   E
'Twill all be forgotten a hundred years hence. *Chorus*

The Boston Come-All-Ye

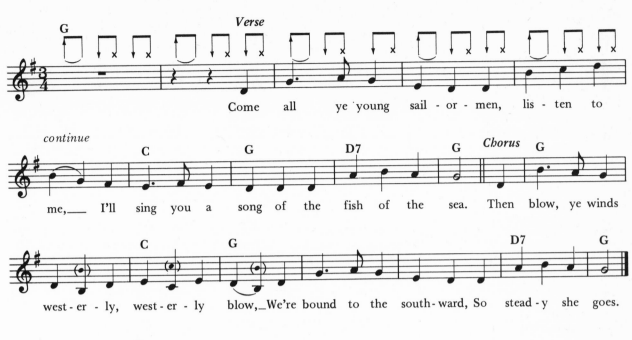

Come all ye young sail-or-men, lis-ten to me,— I'll sing you a song of the fish of the sea. Then blow, ye winds west-er-ly, west-er-ly blow,—We're bound to the south-ward, So stead-y she goes.

     G
Oh, first come the whale, the biggest of all,

  C   G   D7   G
He clumb up aloft and let every sail fall. *Chorus*

     G
And next come the mackerel with his striped back,

  C   G   D7   G
He hauled aft the sheets and he boarded each tack. *Chorus*

 G
Then come the porpoise with his short snout,

  C   G   D7   G
He went to the wheel, calling, "Ready! About!" *Chorus*

 G
Then come the smelt, the smallest of all,

  C   G   D7   G
He jumped to the poop and sung out, "Topsail, haul!" *Chorus*

     G
The herring came saying, "I'm king of the seas,

   C   G   D7   G
If you want any wind I will blow you a breeze." *Chorus*

 G
Next come the codfish with his chuckle-head,

  C   G   D7   G
He went to the main-chains to heave at the lead. *Chorus*

 G
Last come the flounder, as flat as the ground,

    C   G   D7   G
Saying, "Damn your eyes, chuckle-head, mind how you sound!" *Chorus*

The Streets of Laredo

As I _____ walked out in the streets of La-

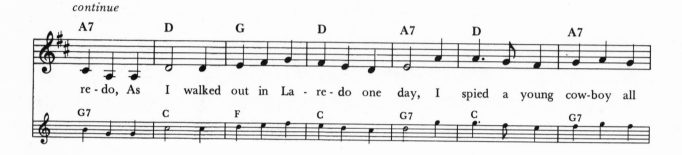

re-do, As I walked out in La-re-do one day, I spied a young cow-boy all

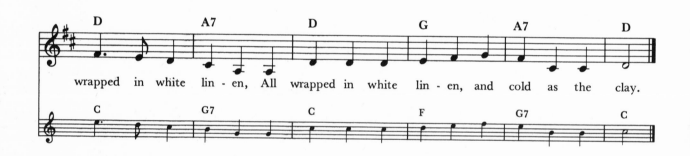

wrapped in white lin-en, All wrapped in white lin-en, and cold as the clay.

     D   A7   D   A7
"I see by your outfit that you are a cowboy,"

     D   G   D   A7
These words he did say as I boldly walked by.

       D   A7   D   A7
"Come sit down beside me and hear my sad story,

     D   G   A7   D
I'm shot in the breast and I know I must die."

       D   A7   D   A7
"It was once in the saddle I used to go dashing,

D   G   D   A7
Once in the saddle I used to go gay;

D   A7   D   A7
First down to Rosie's and then to the card-house—

     D   G   A7   D
Got shot in the breast and I'm dying today."

          D   A7   D   A7
"Get sixteen gamblers to carry my coffin,
      D   G   D   A7
Let six jolly cowboys come sing me a song.
        D   A7   D   A7
Take me to the graveyard and lay the sod o'er me,
      D   G   A7   D
For I'm a young cowboy and I know I've done wrong."

          D   A7   D   A7
"Oh, beat the drum slowly and play the fife lowly,
D   G   D   A7
Play the dead march as you carry me along.
        D   A7   D   A7
Put bunches of roses all over my coffin,
D   G   A7   D
Roses to deaden the clods as they fall." *Repeat Verse One*

CHAPTER FIVE

LOTS MORE CHORDS

Any Number Can Play

Up to now we have played songs with three chords—chords whose relationship to the key have been I, IV and V. In C that has meant C, F and G7. In G—G, C and D7. As you know, moving the capo to different frets has not affected this I, IV, V system.

There are, however, a great number of songs which are harmonized by chords *other* than I, IV and V. Chords can be built on all the twelve notes of the "chromatic scale." That is, any note at any fret of the banjo (or any key—black or white—of the piano) may be the starting point, or "root" of a great number of chords. These chords may be called "major"—as in C, F and G. They may be called "dominant seventh"—as in G7 and D7. There are other types of chords, as well: "minor," "minor seventh," "diminished," to name but a few.

We will present in this chapter a number of songs with some of these "new" chords. They will all be written in either C or G. You may have to transpose some of them in order to sing them comfortably. Use your capo freely.

As an aid to transposing from C-tuning keys to G-tuning keys, and vice versa, you will find a helpful table on page 98. (For example, a song in C may be too high for you and you may want to sing it in B♭ or A.)

G Tuning

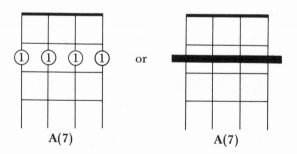

If just the first four strings are played this chord is properly referred to as "A major." It is made up of the notes A, C♯, E. However, when played with the banjo strum, the fifth string (G) is added to the total sound—giving us A7.

Lonesome Valley

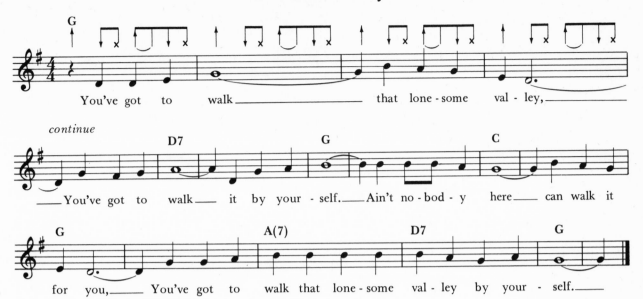

You've got to walk_____ that lone-some val-ley,_____

continue

D7 _You've got to walk__ it by your-self.__ **G** Ain't no-bod-y **C** here__ can walk it

G for you,____ You've got to walk that lone-some **A(7)** val-ley by **D7** your-self.__ **G**

G
Your mother's got to walk that lonesome valley,

D7   **G**
She's got to walk it by herself.

C   **G**
Ain't nobody else can walk it for her—

A(7)   **D7**   **G**
She's got to walk that lonesome valley by herself.

G
Your father's got to walk that lonesome valley,

D7   **G**
He's got to walk it by himself.

C   **G**
Ain't nobody else can walk it for him—

A(7)   **D7**   **G**
He's got to walk that lonesome valley by himself.

G
Everybody's got to walk that lonesome valley,

D7   **G**
They got to walk it by themselves.

C   **G**
Ain't nobody else can walk it for them—

A(7)   **D7**   **G**
They got to walk that lonesome valley by themselves.

G
If you cannot preach like Peter,

D7   **G**
If you cannot pray like Paul,

C   **G**
You can tell the love of Jesus—

A(7) D7   **G**
You can say   He died for all. *Repeat Verse One*

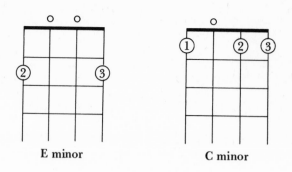

E minor   C minor

Please note that *Home on the Range* is in $\frac{3}{4}$ time.

Home on the Range

Oh, give me a home where the buf-fa-lo roam, Where the deer and the an-te-lope play.___ Where sel-dom is heard a dis-cour-ag-ing word, And the skies are not cloud-y all day.___

Chorus
Home, home on the range,___ Where the deer and the an-te-lope play,___ Where sel-dom is heard a dis-cour-ag-ing word, And the skies are not cloud-y all day.___

```
        G                          C
How often at night when the heavens are bright
        G              A(7)       D7
With the light from the glittering stars,
        G                          C
Have I stood there amazed and asked as I gazed,
        G        D7           G
If their glory exceeds that of ours. *Chorus*


            G                    C
Where the air is so pure, the zephyrs so free,
        G          A(7)       D7
The breezes so balmy and light,
        G                          C
That I would not exchange my home on the range
        G        D7         G
For all the cities so bright. *Chorus*


            G                        C
Oh, I love those wild flow'rs in this dear land of ours,
        G          A(7)       D7
The curlew, I love to hear scream,
        G                          C
And I love the white rocks and the antelope flocks,
        G          D7          G
That graze on the mountaintops green. *Chorus*
```

The fifth string is not always acceptable musically with every chord. When this is the case, as with B7, just leave out the thumb-stroke.

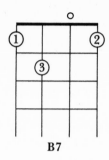

B7

John Brown's Body

Play downstrokes only for this march.

Verse
G
continue
C

John Brown's bod - y lies a - mould - 'ring in his grave, John Brown's bod - y lies a-

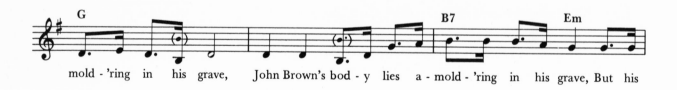

G   B7   Em

mold - 'ring in his grave, John Brown's bod - y lies a - mold - 'ring in his grave, But his

C   D7   G   **Chorus** G   C

soul goes march - ing on. Glo - ry, glo - ry, hal - le - lu - jah, Glo - ry, glo - ry, hal - le -

G   B7   Em   C   D7   G

lu - jah, Glo - ry, glo - ry, hal - le - lu - jah, His soul goes march - ing on.

72

G
He captured Harper's Ferry with his nineteen men so true,

    C   G
And he frightened old Virginia till she trembled through and through.

                                   B7   Em
They hung him for a traitor, they themselves the traitor crew,

         C   D7   G
But his soul goes marching on! *Chorus*

G
John Brown died that the slave might be free,

C   G
John Brown died that the slave might be free,

                       B7   Em
John Brown died that the slave might be free,

         C   D7   G
And his soul goes marching on. *Chorus*

      G
The stars of heaven are looking kindly down,

     C   G
The stars of heaven are looking kindly down,

              B7   Em
The stars of heaven are looking kindly down

         C   D7   G
On the grave of old John Brown. *Chorus*

G
Now has come the glorious jubilee,

C   G
Now has come the glorious jubilee,

              B7   Em
Now has come the glorious jubilee,

         C   D7   G
When all mankind is free. *Chorus*

Don't play the fifth string along with E7. With the A minor chord you may include it.

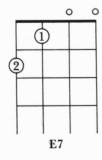

E7

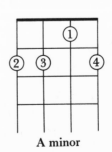

A minor

Landlord, Fill the Flowing Bowl

Land - lord, fill the flow - ing bowl un - til it doth run o - ver,

Land - lord, fill the flow - ing bowl un - til it doth run o - ver.

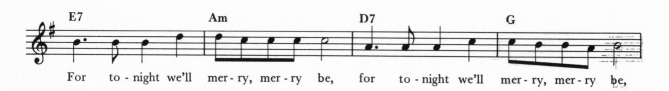

For to - night we'll mer - ry, mer - ry be, for to - night we'll mer - ry, mer - ry be,

for to - night we'll mer - ry, mer - ry be, To - mor - row we'll be so - ber.

     G   Em   D7   G
The man who drinks good whisky clear and goes to bed right mellow,
                  Em   D7   G
The man who drinks good whisky clear and goes to bed right mellow,
E7   Am   D7   G   Em   Am
Lives as he ought to live, lives as he ought to live, lives as he ought to live,
    D7   G
And dies a happy fellow.

     G   Em   D7   G
The man who drinks cold water pure and goes to bed quite sober,
                  Em   D7   G
The man who drinks cold water pure and goes to bed quite sober,
E7   Am   D7   G
Falls as the leaves do fall, falls as the leaves do fall, falls as the leaves do fall.
    D7   G
So early in October.

     G   Em   D7   G
The man who drinks just what he likes and getteth "half seas over,"
                  Em   D7   G
The man who drinks just what he likes and getteth "half seas over,"
E7   Am   D7   G   Em   Am
Lives until he dies—perhaps, lives until he dies—perhaps, lives until he dies—perhaps,
    D7   G
And then lies down in clover.

> G   Em   D7   G
> The little girl who gets a kiss, and runs to tell her mother,
>
>   Em   D7   G
> The little girl who gets a kiss, and runs to tell her mother,
>
> E7   Am   D7   G   Em   Am
> Does a very foolish thing, does a very foolish thing, does a very foolish thing,
>
>   D7   G
> And seldom gets another.

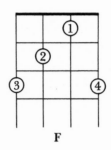

F

Little Maggie

Where is lit - tle Mag - gie? Oh, yon - der there she stands. She's_

drink - ing down her lik - ker with a low - down sor - ry man.

G   F
Oh, how can I stand it,
G   F   G
To see those two blue eyes.

                 F
They're shining like two diamonds,
G   F   G
Two diamonds in the sky.

G   F
Sometimes I have a nickel,
G   F   G
Sometimes I have a dime.

              F
Sometimes I have ten dollars,
G   F   G
To buy Little Maggie wine.

G   F
Pretty flowers were made for blooming,
G   F   G
Pretty stars were meant to shine.

                 F
Pretty girls were meant for boys to love,
G   F   G
Little Maggie was made for mine.

G   F
She's marching to the station,
G   F   G
Got a suitcase in her hand.

              F
She is going for to leave me,
G   F   G
She's bound for some distant land.

With B minor you may want to eliminate the fifth string sometimes. It is not always objectionable. See how you like it here.

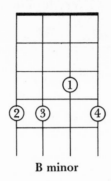

B minor

Home in That Rock

Capo recommended on 3rd fret. What key would that be?

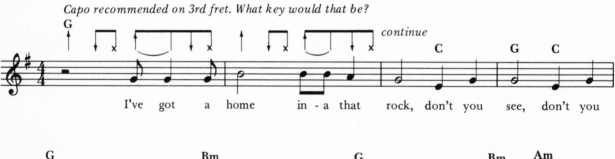

I've got a home in - a that rock, don't you see, don't you

see? I've got a home in - a that rock don't you see, don't you

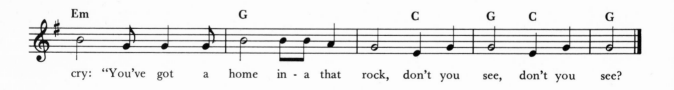

see? Be - tween the earth and sky, Thought I heard my Sav - ior

cry: "You've got a home in - a that rock, don't you see, don't you see?

       G   C   G   C   G

Poor man Lazarus, poor as I, don't you see? Don't you see?

            Bm   G   Bm Am   D7

Poor man Lazarus, poor as I, don't you see? Don't you see?

         G

Poor man Lazarus, poor as I,

           Bm   Em

When he died he found a home on high.

          G   C   G   C   G

He had a home in-a that rock, don't you see? Don't you see?

          G   C   G   C   G

Rich man Dives lived so well, don't you see? Don't you see?

            Bm   G   Bm Am   D7

Rich man Dives lived so well, don't you see? Don't you see?

         G

Rich man Dives, he lived so well,

           Bm   Em

When he died he found a home in hell.

          G   C   G   C   G

Had no home in-a that rock, don't you see? Don't you see?

            G   C   G   C   G

God gave Noah the rainbow sign, don't you see? Don't you see?

            Bm   G   Bm Am   D7

God gave Noah the rainbow sign, don't you see? Don't you see?

           G

God gave Noah the rainbow sign,

           Bm   Em

"No more water, but fire next time."

          G   C   G   C   G

He had a home in-a that rock, don't you see? Don't you see?

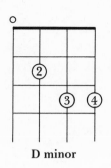

D minor

Darling Cory

Capo recommended on 2nd fret. What key would that be?

Wake up, wake up, dar-ling Cor-y,___ What makes you sleep___ so sound? The___

rev-en-ue of-fi-cers are com-in',___ For to tear your still___ house down.___

G
The first time I saw darling Cory,

She was standing by the banks of the sea.

Dm
Had two pistols strapped 'round her body,
G
And a banjo on her knee.

G
Go 'way from me, darling Cory,

Quit hanging 'round my bed.

Dm
Pretty women run me distracted.
G
Corn likker's killed me dead.

G
Last night as I lay on my pillow,

Last night as I lay on my bed.

Dm
Last night as I lay on my pillow,
G
I dreamed darling Cory was dead.

G
The last time I saw darling Cory,

She had a wine glass in her hand.

Dm
She was drinking that cold pizen likker
G
With a low-down sorry man.

G
Go and dig me a hole in the meadow,

A hole in the cold cold ground.

Dm
Go and dig me a hole in the meadow,
G
Just to lay darling Cory down.

G
Don't you hear them bluebirds singing?

Don't you hear that mournful sound?

Dm
They're preaching Cory's funeral
G
In the lonesome burying ground.

C Tuning

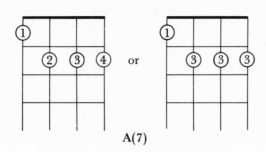

or

A(7)

If just the first four strings are played this chord is properly referred to as "A major." It is made up of the notes A, C♯, E. However, when played with the banjo strum, the fifth string (G) is added to the total sound—giving us A7.

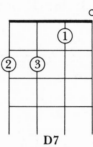

D7

Salty Dog

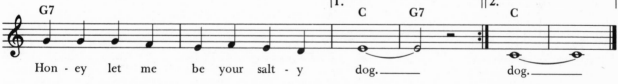

The verses are sung to the first eight measures of the chorus.

C   A(7)
Down in the wildwood, sitting on a log,
D7
Singing a song about a salty dog.
    G7   C
    Honey, let me be your salty dog. *Chorus*

C   A(7)
Two old maids a-sitting in the sand,
D7
Each one wishing that the other was a man.
    G7   C
    Honey, let me be your salty dog. *Chorus*

C   A(7)
Worst day I ever had in my life,
D7
When my best friend caught me kissing his wife.
    G7   C
    Honey, let me be your salty dog. *Chorus*

C   A(7)
God made a woman and He made her mighty funny,
D7
When you kiss her 'round the mouth, just as sweet

      as any honey.
    G7   C
    Honey, let me be your salty dog. *Chorus*

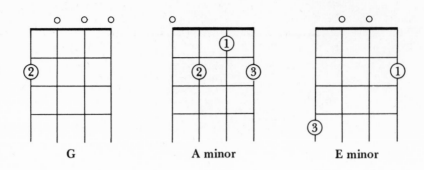

G   A minor   E minor

"Sweet Betsy from Pike" is in $\frac{3}{4}$ time.

Sweet Betsy from Pike

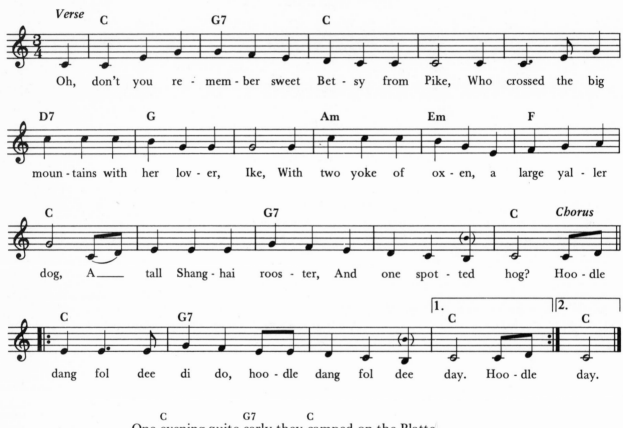

Verse

Oh, don't you re-mem-ber sweet Bet-sy from Pike, Who crossed the big
moun-tains with her lov-er, Ike, With two yoke of ox-en, a large yal-ler
dog, A___ tall Shang-hai roos-ter, And one spot-ted hog? Hoo-dle
dang fol dee di do, hoo-dle dang fol dee day. Hoo-dle day.

            C   G7   C
One evening quite early they camped on the Platte,
                  D7   G
'Twas near by the road on a green shady flat,
          Am   Em   F   C
Where Betsy, sore-footed, lay down to repose—
                G7   C
With wonder Ike gazed on his Pike County rose. *Chorus*

            C   G7   C
The Shanghai ran off and their cattle all died,
                  D7   G
That morning the last piece of bacon was fried.
          Am   Em   F   C
Poor Ike was discouraged and Betsy got mad,
                G7   C
The dog drooped his tail and looked wondrously sad. *Chorus*

```
        C              G7        C
They soon reached the desert where Betsy gave out,
                    D7            G
And down in the sand she lay rolling about.
      Am          Em            F      C
While Ike, half distracted, looked on in surprise,
                    G7                       C
Saying, "Betsy, get up, you'll get sand in your eyes." Chorus


            C         G7      C
Sweet Betsy got up in a great deal of pain,
                    D7          G
Declared she'd go back to Pike County again.
      Am        Em          F      C
But Ike gave a sigh and they fondly embraced,
                    G7                       C
And they traveled along with his arm 'round her waist. Chorus


C              G7          C
Out on the desert one bright starry night,
                    D7        G
They broke out the whisky and Betsy got tight.
      Am            Em        F          C
She laughed and she shouted and danced o'er the plain,
                    G7                       C
And showed her bare arse to the whole wagon train. Chorus


        C              G7        C
Long Ike and Sweet Betsy attended a dance,
            D7        G
Ike wore a pair of his Pike County pants.
      Am          Em        F        C
Sweet Betsy was dressed up in ribbons and rings,
                    G7                       C
Quoth Ike, "You're an angel, but where are your wings?" Chorus


      C            G7            C
A miner said, "Betsy, will you dance with me?"
                  D7          G
"I will, you old hoss, if you don't make too free.
      Am          Em        F            C
But don't dance me hard, do you want to know why?
                G7                    C
Doggone ye, I'm chock full of strong alkali!" Chorus


            C          G7        C
Long Ike and Sweet Betsy were married, of course.
                D7        G
But Ike, growing jealous, obtained a divorce.
      Am        Em        F        C
And Betsy, well satisfied, said with a shout,
                G7                          C
"Goodbye, you big lummox, I'm glad you backed out!" Chorus
```

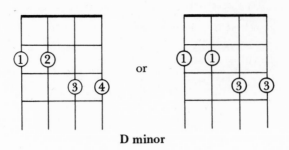

D minor

Michael, Row the Boat Ashore

Mich - ael, row the boat a - shore, Hal - le - lu - jah, Mich - ael, row the boat a - shore, Hal - le - lu - jah.

C
Sister, help to trim the sail,
F C
Hallelu-jah,
Em   Dm
Sister, help to trim the sail,
C G7 C
Hallelu-u-jah. *Chorus*

C
Jordan's River is chilly and cold,
F C
Hallelu-jah,
Em   Dm
Chills the body but warms the soul,
C G7 C
Hallelu-u-jah. *Chorus*

C
Michael's boat is a gospel boat,
F C
Hallelu-jah,
Em   Dm
Michael's boat is a gospel boat,
C G7 C
Hallelu-u-jah. *Chorus*

C
Jordan's River is deep and wide,
F C
Hallelu-jah,
Em   Dm
Meet my mother on the other side,
C G7 C
Hallelu-u-jah. *Chorus*

C
If you get there before I do,
F C
Hallelu-jah,
Em   Dm
Tell my people I'm coming, too,
C G7 C
Hallelu-u-jah. *Chorus*

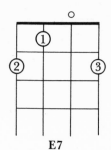

Don't play the 5th string along with E7.

Railroad Bill

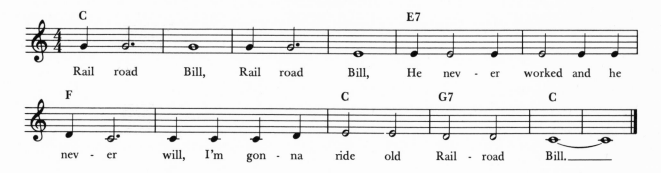

Rail road Bill, Rail road Bill, He nev - er worked and he nev - er will, I'm gon - na ride old Rail - road Bill._____

C
Railroad Bill, he was a mighty mean man,
E7   F
Shot the midnight lantern out the brakeman's hand.
            C   G7   C
    I'm gonna ride old Railroad Bill.

C
Railroad Bill took my wife,
        E7   F
Said, if I didn't like it he would take my life.
            C   G7   C
    I'm gonna ride old Railroad Bill.

C
Going up on the mountain, going out west,
    E7   F
"Thirty-eight special" sticking out of my vest.
            C   G7   C
    I'm gonna ride old Railroad Bill.

C
I've got a "thirty-eight special" on a "forty-four" frame,
E7   F
How can I miss him when I've got dead aim?
            C   G7   C
    I'm gonna ride old Railroad Bill.

C
Buy me a pistol just as long as my arm,
E7   F
Kill everybody ever done me harm.
            C   G7   C
    I'm gonna ride old Railroad Bill.

C
Honey, honey, honey, think I'm a fool,
E7   F
Think I would quit you when the weather's cool?
            C   G7   C
    I'm gonna ride old Railroad Bill.

83

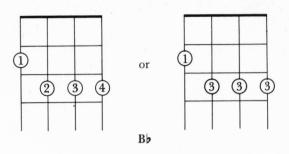

Bb

Old Joe Clark

Verse
C

Old Joe Clark, the preach-er's son, Preached all ov-er the plain, The

on-ly text he ev-er knew was "High, low, jack, and the game."

Chorus
C

'Round and a-round, old Joe Clark, 'Round and a-round I say, He'd

fol-ler me ten thou-sand miles to hear my ban-jo play.

C
I used to live on the mountain top,

But now I live in town.

I'm boarding at the big hotel,
Bb   C
Courting Betsy Brown. *Chorus*

C
Old Joe had a yellow cat,

She'd neither sing nor pray.

She stuck her head in a buttermilk jar
Bb   C
And washed her sins away. *Chorus*

C
Old Joe Clark, he had a house,

Fifteen storeys high,

And every storey in that house
Bb   C
Was filled with chicken pie. *Chorus*

C
I would not marry an old maid,

Tell you the reason why,

Her neck's so long and stringy, boys,
Bb   C
'Fraid she'd never die. *Chorus*

C
Wish I had a sweetheart,

I'd set her on the shelf,

And every time she'd smile at me,
Bb   C
I'd get up there myself. *Chorus*

Minor and Modal Keys

There are a number of different scales (or modes) whose tonic (I) chord is a minor chord. Not every song whose tonic is a minor chord is necessarily in a minor key. For an exact determination of what key a piece of music is in one must examine the notes of the scale that make up that piece. More particularly, attention must be paid to the *intervals* between those notes. An *interval* is the musical distance between two notes. It is measured in *half steps*. A half step is played on the banjo by moving from one fret to the nearest neighboring fret (up or down). On the piano a half step is played by moving from one key to the nearest neighboring key.

Without going into any more detail at this point, suffice it to say that there are three types of minor scales (*natural, harmonic, melodic*) and at least two modes (*pentatonic, dorian*) commonly encountered whose tonic chord will be a minor chord. For our purposes here we may lump these five differing scale patterns together under the general heading of "minor keys."

C Tuning

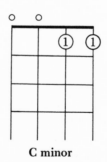

C minor

Nine Hundred Miles

Verse

Cm

I'm a - rid - ing on this train, I've got tears in my eyes, Try'n' to read a

let - ter from my home.___ If this train runs me right, I'll be home by Sat - ur - day

Bb   Cm   Chorus

night, 'Cause I'm nine - hun - dred miles from___ my home.____ And I

G7   1. Cm   2. Cm

hate to hear that lone - some whis - tle blow.___ It's that
long and lone - some train a whis - tlin'   down.___

Cm
Well, the train I ride on is a hundred coaches long,

You can hear the whistle blow a hundred miles.

And the lonesome whistle call is the mournfullest of all,
      Bb   Cm
'Cause it's nine hundred miles from my home. *Chorus*

Cm
Well, I'll pawn you my watch and I'll pawn you my chain,

Pawn you my gold diamond ring.

If that train runs me right I'll be home Saturday night,
      Bb   Cm
'Cause I'm nine hundred miles from my home. *Chorus*

Cm
If my woman says so, I'll railroad no more,

But I'll sidetrack that wheeler and go home.

If that train runs me right I'll be home Saturday night,
      Bb   Cm
'Cause it's nine hundred miles from my home. *Chorus*

86

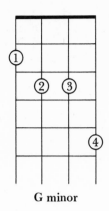

G minor

What Shall We Do with the Drunken Sailor?

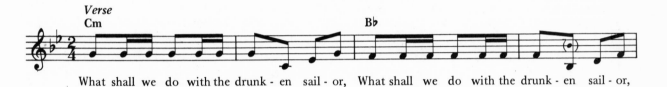

Verse
Cm .... Bb

What shall we do with the drunk - en sail - or, What shall we do with the drunk - en sail - or,

Cm .... Gm ... Cm

What shall we do with the drunk - en sail - or, Ear - lye in the morn - ing?

Chorus:
Cm
Hooray, and up she rises,

Bb
Hooray, and up she rises,

Cm
Hooray, and up she rises,

Gm   Cm
Earlye in the morning.

Cm
Put him in the long boat till he's sober,

Bb
Put him in the long boat till he's sober,

Cm
Put him in the long boat till he's sober,

Gm   Cm
Earlye in the morning. *Chorus*

Cm
Put him in the scuppers with a hosepipe on him,

Bb
Put him in the scuppers with a hosepipe on him,

Cm
Put him in the scuppers with a hosepipe on him,

Gm   Cm
Earlye in the morning. *Chorus*

Cm
Heave him by the leg in a running bowline,

Bb
Heave him by the leg in a running bowline,

Cm
Heave him by the leg in a running bowline,

Gm   Cm
Earlye in the morning. *Chorus*

Cm
Hang him by the ears till his eyeballs fall out,

Bb
Hang him by the ears till his eyeballs fall out,

Cm
Hang him by the ears till his eyeballs fall out,

Gm   Cm
Earlye in the morning. *Chorus*

Cm
That's what we'll do with the drunken sailor,

Bb
That's what we'll do with the drunken sailor,

Cm
That's what we'll do with the drunken sailor,

Gm   Cm
Earlye in the morning. *Chorus*

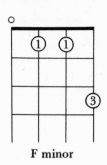

F minor

Joshua Fought the Battle of Jericho

Chorus

Josh-ua fought the bat-tle of Jer-i-cho,— Jer-i-cho,— Jer-i-cho,_____

Fine
(The end)

Josh-ua fought the bat-tle of Jer-i-cho,— And the walls came tum-bl-ing down.

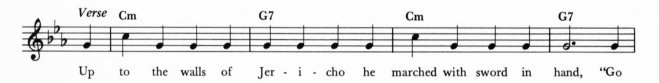

Verse

Up to the walls of Jer-i-cho he marched with sword in hand, "Go

to chorus

blow them ram horns!" Josh-u-a cried, "'Cause the bat-tle is in my hand." That morn-ing.

Cm   G7
Then the lamb, ram, sheep horns began to blow,

Cm   G7
Trumpets began to sound.

Cm
Joshua commanded the children to shout,

G7   Cm
And the walls came tumbling down,

That morning! *Chorus*

Cm   G7
There's no man like Joshua,

Cm   G7
No man like Saul.

Cm
No man like Joshua

G7   Cm
At the battle of Jericho,

That morning! *Chorus*

In order to play the E-flat chord you must cover all four strings at the third fret with the first finger and then add the other fingers as shown on the diagram. Press down hard enough to get a clear sound on the four strings before you add the other two fingers. This is called playing a *barre*. It is a very important technique. There are a great many barre chords. In the chord diagrams a barre may be indicated either by a solid line or by a series of encircled numeral ones across the desired fret.

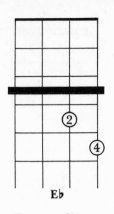

Eb

Peter Gray

Verse Cm
Once on a time there lived a man, His name was Pet-er Gray,— He

G7   Cm
lived way down in that there town called— Penn-syl-van-i - ay.

Chorus Cm
Blow, ye winds in the morn - ing, Blow, ye winds, hi ho,

Eb   Cm

G7   Cm
Blow, ye winds in the morn - ing, And blow, blow, blow.

Cm
Now, Peter fell in love all with

G7   Cm
A nice young girl.

The first two letters of her name

G7   Cm
Were Luc-i-anna Quirl. *Chorus*

Cm
Just as they were a-going to wed,

G7   Cm
Her father did say no;

And quin-ci-contly she was sent

G7   Cm
Beyond the O-hi-o. *Chorus*

Cm
When Peter heard his love was lost,

G7   Cm
He knew not what to say.

He'd half a mind to jump into

G7   Cm
The Susquehan-i-ay. *Chorus*

Cm
But he went traveling to the west

G7   Cm
For furs and other skins;

Till he was caught and scalp-i-ed

G7   Cm
By blood-i In-ji-ins. *Chorus*

Cm
When Luc-i-anna heard the news,

G7   Cm
She straightway took to bed,

And never did get up again

G7   Cm
Until she di-i-ed. *Chorus*

Cm
You fathers all a warning take—

G7   Cm
Each one as has a girl;

And think upon poor Peter Gray

G7   Cm
And Luc-i-anna Quirl. *Chorus*

89

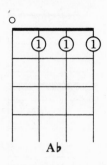

Ab

Drill, Ye Tarriers, Drill

Verse

Cm   G7

Ev - 'ry morn - ing at sev - en o' - clock there's__ twen - ty tar - ri - ers a

Cm

work - ing at the rock, And the boss comes a - round and he says, "Keep still, And

G7   Cm   G7   Cm

come down heav - y on the cast iron drill." And drill, ye tar - ri - ers, drill.

Chorus

Cm   Bb   Cm

Drill, ye tar - ri - ers, drill. And it's work all day for the su - gar in your tay,

G7   Cm   G7   Cm   Ab   Cm

Down be - hind the rail - way, And drill, ye tar - ri - ers, drill, and blast, and fire.

Cm
Our new foreman was Jim McCann,
G7
By God, he was a blame mean man.
Cm
Last week a premature blast went off,
G7
And a mile in the air went big Jim Goff,
Cm   G7   Cm
And drill, ye tarriers, drill. *Chorus*

Cm
The next time payday come around,
G7
Jim Goff a dollar short was found.
Cm
When he asked what for, come this reply,
G7
"Yer docked fer the time you wuz up in the sky!"
Cm   G7   Cm
And drill, ye tarriers, drill. *Chorus*

Cm
The boss was a fine man down to the ground,
G7
And he married a lady six-foot 'round.
Cm
She baked good bread and she baked it well,
G7
But she baked it hard as the holes in hell,
Cm   G7   Cm
And drill, ye tarriers, drill. *Chorus*

G Minor Tuning

The banjo really sounds its best when the tonic chord—whatever the key—is played with the maximum number of open strings. Chords with open strings also permit the left hand to move around more freely in the playing of the melody. We haven't gone into that as yet—but don't worry, it's coming!

To play in the key of G minor in the usual G (major) tuning would turn out to be very awkward and unsatisfying. In the G tuning the G minor chord would be played somewhat as in the C tuning. This would force your left hand to be locked onto the third and fifth frets:

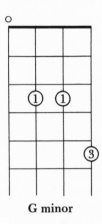

G minor

While it is perfectly reasonable to be expected to play this chord if it ever crops up in the key of G or C, there is a much better way to get it when G minor is the tonic. We retune the banjo to an open G minor chord.

This is gotten very simply by lowering the second string one half step from B to B-flat. If you play the third fret of the third (G) string you will get the note B-flat. This note should guide you in the retuning of the second string. Now, of course, our G minor chord looks like this:

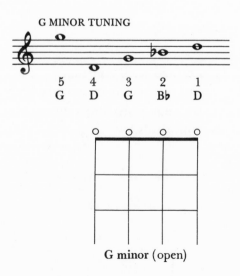

G minor (open)

The fingering of all the chords that you have already learned in the G tuning would have to be altered slightly to compensate for the one changed string. You merely raise whatever note falls on the second string *one fret*. This will make up for the lowering of that string by one half step. Simple?

For example, here are four chords which you have already played in the G tuning. These are chords which often occur in G minor. Note that the only thing new about them is what happens on the second string.

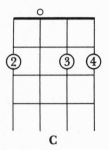

C

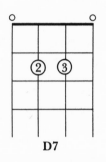

D7

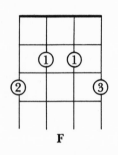

F

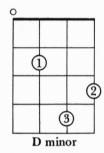

D minor

And here are another three commonly found chords in G minor.

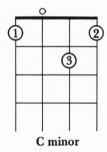

C minor

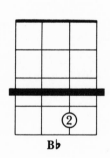

Bb

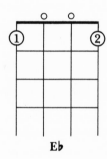

Eb

Now, if you like, you can go back and transpose the songs that we have just done in C minor. Perhaps some of them will be more suited to your vocal range in G minor or a G minor derivative like A minor. (See page 98 for the table of transposing equivalents.)

The Ox Driving Song

Sing an octave lower than written. Use a capo if necessary.

I pop my whip and I bring the blood, I make my lead - ers

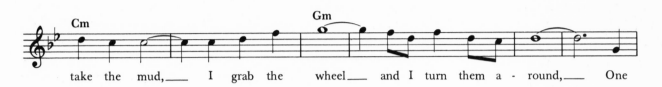

take the mud,___ I grab the wheel___ and I turn them a - round,___ One

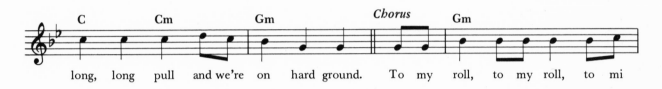

long, long pull and we're on hard ground. To my roll, to my roll, to mi

ri - dee - o, to my roll, to my roll, to my ri - dee - o,___ To my ri - dee - o,___

___ To my ru - dee - o,___ To my roll, to my roll, to my ri - dee - o.

Gm
On the fourteenth day of October-o,
C   Cm
I hitched my team in order-o.
Gm
To drive to the hills of Saludio.
C   Cm   Gm
To my roll, to my roll, to my ride-e-o. *Chorus*

Gm
When I got there the hills were steep,
C   Cm
A tender-hearted person'd weep
Gm
To hear me cuss and pop my whip,
C   Cm Gm
To see my oxen pull and slip. *Chorus*

Gm
When I get home I'll have revenge,
C   Cm
I'll land my family among my friends.
Gm
I'll bid adieu to the whip and line,
C   Cm   Gm
And drive no more in the wintertime. *Chorus*

Buffalo Skinners

Sing an octave lower than written. Use a capo if necessary.

Come all you old-time cow-boys, and lis-ten to my song,

Please do not grow wear-y, I'll not de-tain you long, Con-

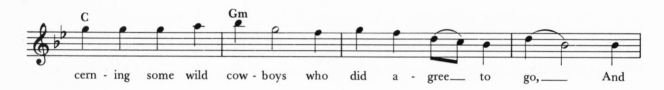

cern-ing some wild cow-boys who did a-gree__ to go,__ And

spend a sum-mer pleas-ant on the trail of the buf-fa-lo.

Gm   Cm   Gm
I found myself in Texas in the spring of 'eighty-three,
        Eb   Gm   Bb   Gm
When a well-known famous drover come a-walking up to me,
            C   Gm
Saying, "How do you do, young feller, and how would you like to go
        Bb   Dm   Gm   F   Gm
And spend a summer pleasant on the trail of the buffalo?"

                Gm   Cm   Gm
Well, me being out of work right then to the drover I did say,
        Eb   Gm   Bb   Gm
"This going out on the buffalo range depends upon your pay.
            C   Gm
But if you will pay good wages, transportation to and fro,
    Bb   Dm   Gm   F   Gm
I think I might go with you to the range of the buffalo."

                Gm   Cm   Gm
"Of course I'll pay good wages, and transportation, too,
        Eb   Gm   Bb   Gm
If you'll agree to work for me until the season's through.
            C   Gm
But if you should grow weary and decide to run away,
        Bb   Dm   Gm F   Gm
You'll starve to death out on the trail and also lose your pay."

94

<pre>
  Gm   Cm   Gm
With all this flattering talking he signed up quite a train.
    Eb   Gm   Bb   Gm
Some ten or twelve in number—some able-bodied men.
        C   Gm
Our trip it was a pleasant one as we hit the westward road,
     Bb   Dm   Gm   F   Gm
And then we crossed old Boggy Creek in old New Mexico.

      Gm   Cm   Gm
Well, there our pleasures ended and our troubles all begun.
    Eb   Gm   Bb   Gm
A lightning storm did hit us and made our cattle run.
  C   Gm
Got all full of stickers from the cactus that did grow,
     Bb   Dm   Gm   F   Gm
And outlaws waiting to pick us off on the trail of the buffalo.

        Gm   Cm   Gm
Well, the working season ended and the drover would not pay.
    Eb   Gm   Bb   Gm
"You all have drunk too much. You're all in debt to me!"
        C   Gm
But the cowboys never had heard of such a thing as the bankrupt law,
     Bb   Dm   Gm   F   Gm
So we left that drover's bones to bleach on the trail of the buffalo.
</pre>

E Minor to G Major: A Special Case

Some banjo tunes which seem to be in E minor never have any other chord than G major. (In general terms this would be *I minor* and *III major*. Other pairs are A minor and C major, D minor and F major, G minor and Bb major, C minor and Eb major, etc.)

These chords are best fingered in the G major tuning with an open G chord and the E minor you already know.

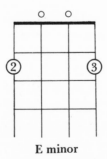

E minor

You get a nice hammer-on on the second frets of the fourth and first strings (one at a time, that is).

Pretty Polly

I court-ed Pret-ty Pol - ly the live-long—night, I court-ed Pret-ty Pol - ly the

live - long—night, Then killed her next morn - ing be - fore it was light.

Em
"Pretty Polly, pretty Polly, come and go along with me,
G
Pretty Polly, pretty Polly, come and go along with me,
Em
Before we get married, some pleasure to see."

Em
She got on up behind him and away they did go,
G
She got on up behind him and away they did go,
Em
Over the mountains and valleys so low.

Em
They rode a little bit further and what did they spy?
G
They rode a little bit further and what did they spy?
Em
But a new dug grave and a spade lying by.

Em
"Oh, Willie, sweet Willie, I'm afraid of your ways,
G
Willie, sweet Willie, I'm afraid of your ways,
Em
I'm afraid you will lead my poor body astray."

Em
"Pretty Polly, pretty Polly, you're guessing just right,
G
Pretty Polly, pretty Polly, you're guessing just right,
Em
I dug on your grave better part of last night."

Em
Then from pretty Polly the tears began to swell,

G
Then from pretty Polly the tears began to swell,

Em
"Have pity on me and your infant as well."

Em
He stabbed his knife into her, her life's blood did flow,

G
He stabbed his knife into her, her life's blood did flow,

Em
And into her grave pretty Polly did go.

Em
He threw a little dirt over her and started for home,

G
He threw a little dirt over her and started for home,

Em
Leaving no one behind but the wild birds to mourn.

Em
A debt to the Devil, sweet Willie must pay,

G
A debt to the Devil, sweet Willie must pay,

Em
For killing pretty Polly and running away.

The following Transposing Tables list in handy reference form all the chords we have learned to date and their equivalents in other keys.

G Major or G Minor Tuning

Key	Capo	I	II	Flat III	III	IV	V	Flat VI	VI	Flat VII
G, Gm	0	G, Gm	A7, Am	Bb	B7, Bm	C, Cm	D7, Dm	Eb	E7, Em	F
Ab, Abm	1	Ab, Abm	Bb7, Bbm	Cb = B	C7, Cm	Db, Dbm	Eb7, Ebm	Fb = E	F7, Fm	Gb
A, Am	2	A, Am	B7, Bm	C	C#7, C#m	D, Dm	E7, Em	F	F#7, F#m	G
Bb, Bbm	3	Bb, Bbm	C7, Cm	Db	D7, Dm	Eb, Ebm	F7, Fm	Gb	G7, Gm	Ab
B, Bm	4	B, Bm	C#7, C#m	D	D#7, D#m	E, Em	F#7, F#m	G	G#7, G#m	A

C Tuning

Key	Capo	I	II	Flat III	III	IV	V	Flat VI	VI	Flat VII
C, Cm	0	C, Cm	D7, Dm	Eb	E7, Em	F, Fm	G7, Gm	Ab	A7, Am	Bb
Db, Dbm	1	Db, Dbm	Eb7, Ebm	Fb = E	F7, Fm	Gb, Gbm	Ab7, Abm	A	Bb7, Bbm	Cb = B
D, Dm	2	D, Dm	E7, Em	F	F#7, F#m	G, Gm	A7, Am	Bb	B7, Bm	C
Eb, Ebm	3	Eb, Ebm	F7, Fm	Gb	G7, Gm	Ab, Abm	Bb7, Bbm	Cb = B	C7, Cm	Db
E, Em	4	E, Em	F#7, F#m	G	G#7, G#m	A, Am	B7, Bm	C	C#7, C#m	D
F, Fm	5	F, Fm	G7, Gm	Ab	A7, Am	Bb, Bbm	C7, Cm	Db	D7, Dm	Eb
F#, F#m	6	F#, F#m	G#7, G#m	A	A#7, A#m	B, Bm	C#7, C#m	D	D#7, D#m	E
Gb, Gbm	6	Gb, Gbm	Ab7, Abm	Bbb = A	Bb7, Bbm	Cb, Cbm	Db7, Dbm	Ebb = D	Eb7, Ebm	Fb = E

E Minor–G Major (G Tuning)

Key	Capo	I	III
Em	0	Em	G
Fm	1	Fm	Ab
F#m	2	F#m	A
Gm	3	Gm	Bb
G#m (Abm)	4	G#m (Abm)	B (Cb)

CHAPTER SIX

UP THE NECK WITHOUT A CAPO

Movable Chords

A good banjo player must be able to move freely and easily to all positions (frets) on the instrument. Playing in different positions adds interest and variety to accompaniments. It is also absolutely essential for the playing of melody—melody supported by the correct chords at all times.

In order to be able to find your way through this "unknown territory" we have to have a heart to heart talk about the theory of chord construction. Right now.

What Is a Chord? (Funny You Should Ask)

After all the chords you have been playing up to now you probably have formed some vague idea of what a chord is. More than likely you associate chords with diagrams and finger positions. That is all well and good when it comes to remembering where to put your left hand, but it does very little to tell you what you are actually doing and how to figure out other chords in other places.

Chords are constructed along certain simple musical principles, easy to understand and apply.

Major Chords

All major chords are made up of three notes. These notes are in the alphabetical-numerical relationship to each other of 1-3-5.

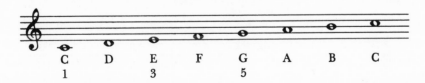

C D E F G A B C
1   3   5

Example: If C = 1, then E = 3 and G = 5.
C E G = C major chord

Example: If F = 1, then A = 3 and C = 5.
F A C = F major chord

Example: If G = 1, then B = 3 and D = 5.
G B D = G major chord

This purely mechanical alphabetical system breaks down, however, if we start on any other note. We need one other vital bit of information: the actual intervals, measured in half steps, between 1 and 3 and 5. Let's take a closer look at a C chord.

$$C \text{ to } C\sharp = \tfrac{1}{2} \text{ step}$$
$$C\sharp \text{ to } D = \tfrac{1}{2} \text{ step}$$
$$D \text{ to } D\sharp = \tfrac{1}{2} \text{ step}$$
$$D\sharp \text{ to } E = \tfrac{1}{2} \text{ step}$$

Therefore, C to E = four half-steps.

$$E \text{ to } F = \tfrac{1}{2} \text{ step}$$
$$F \text{ to } F\sharp = \tfrac{1}{2} \text{ step}$$
$$F\sharp \text{ to } G = \tfrac{1}{2} \text{ step}$$

Therefore, E to G = three half-steps.

If we carried through the same analysis with the F major and G major chords we would come up with exactly the same interval relationships.

We are now in a position to define a major chord definitively.

Major Chord = Note   *Four Half-Steps*   Note   *Three Half-Steps*   Note

Through all this the 1-3-5 alphabetical relationship ("spelling") is maintained.

A   B   C♯   D   E   F♯   G♯   A
1   3   5

Example: If A = 1, then C♯ (not D♭) = 3 and E = 5.
A C♯ E = A-major chord

Minor Chords

All minor chords are made up of three notes. These notes are in the alphabetical-numerical relationship to each other of 1-3-5. But their interval relationship is different from major chords.

E   F♯   G   A   B   C   D   E
1   3   5

Example: If E = 1, then G = 3 and B = 5.
E G B = E minor chord

$$E \text{ to } F = \tfrac{1}{2} \text{ step}$$
$$F \text{ to } F\sharp = \tfrac{1}{2} \text{ step}$$
$$F\sharp \text{ to } G = \tfrac{1}{2} \text{ step}$$

Therefore, E to G = three half-steps.

$$G \ \ to \ \ G\sharp \ = \ \tfrac{1}{2} \ step$$
$$G\sharp \ \ to \ \ A \ \ = \ \tfrac{1}{2} \ step$$
$$A \ \ to \ \ A\sharp \ = \ \tfrac{1}{2} \ step$$
$$A\sharp \ \ to \ \ B \ \ = \ \tfrac{1}{2} \ step$$

Therefore, G to B = four half-steps.

Minor Chord = Note   *Three Half-Steps*   Note   *Four Half-Steps*   Note

Dominant-Seventh Chords

All dominant-seventh chords are made up of four notes. These notes are in the alphabetical-numerical relationship to each other of 1-3-5-7.

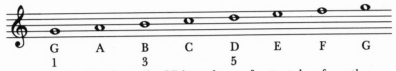

G	A	B	C	D	E	F	G
1		3		5			

(Not a G major scale. G7 is made up of notes taken from the key of C. There is no F♯.)

Example: If G = 1, then B = 3, D = 5 and F = 7.
G B D F = G7 chord

From this we can see that the first three notes of a dominant-seventh chord (1,3,5) form a major chord. It remains just to analyze the interval between 5 and 7.

$$D \ \ to \ \ D\sharp \ = \ \tfrac{1}{2} \ step$$
$$D\sharp \ \ to \ \ E \ \ = \ \tfrac{1}{2} \ step$$
$$E \ \ to \ \ F \ \ = \ \tfrac{1}{2} \ step$$

Therefore, D to F = three half-steps.

Dominant-Seventh Chord = Major Chord   *Three Half-Steps*   Note

There are many other types of chords—chords with differing numbers of notes and interval patterns. We shall restrict ourselves to the three discussed here because they make up the basis of the harmonization of 99.99% of all banjo tunes.

What Does All This Have to Do with the Banjo?

This information, properly assimilated, is of vital importance to all banjo players. The banjo is basically a chord-playing instrument. As a banjo player, chords are your "vocabulary." You must know how to form them, find them and use them.

For reference purposes we will now present tables of the notes of all major, minor and dominant-seventh chords. With this information at hand you will be able to make the connection between theory and practice—between the printed page and the banjo itself.

Major Chords

Chord	1	3	5
A♭(G♯)	A♭(G♯)	C (B♯)	E♭(D♯)
A	A	C♯	E
B♭	B♭	D	F
B	B	D♯	F♯
C	C	E	G
C♯(D♭)	C♯(D♭)	E♯(F)	G♯(A♭)
D	D	F♯	A
E♭	E♭	G	B♭
E	E	G♯	B
F	F	A	C
F♯(G♭)	F♯(G♭)	A♯(B♭)	C♯(D♭)
G	G	B	D

Minor Chords

Chord	1	3	5
A♭m (G♯m)	A♭(G♯)	C♭(B)	E♭(D♯)
Am	A	C	E
B♭m	B♭	D♭	F
Bm	B	D	F♯
Cm	C	E♭	G
C♯m (D♭m)	C♯(D♭)	E (F♭)	G♯(A♭)
Dm	D	F	A
E♭m	E♭	G♭	B♭
Em	E	G	B
Fm	F	A♭	C
F♯m	F♯	A	C♯
Gm	G	B♭	D

Dominant-Seventh Chords

Chord	1	3	5	7
Ab7 (G#7)	Ab(G#)	C (B#)	Eb(D#)	Gb(F#)
A7	A	C#	E	G
Bb7	Bb	D	F	Ab
B7	B	D#	F#	A
C7	C	E	G	Bb
C#7 (Db7)	C#(Db)	E#(F)	G#(Ab)	B (Cb)
D7	D	F#	A	C
Eb7	Eb	G	Bb	Db
E7	E	G#	B	D
F7	F	A	C	Eb
F#7 (Gb7)	F#(Gb)	A#(Bb)	C#(Db)	E (Fb)
G7	G	B	D	F

As I said before, these tables are intended just for reference purposes. Now, here is how you use them. . . .

Inversions—The Missing Link

An *inversion* of a chord is the order of notes, played from lowest to highest. Any of the three notes of a major or minor chord may be written as the lowest. Any of the four notes of a dominant-seventh chord may, likewise, be written as the lowest.

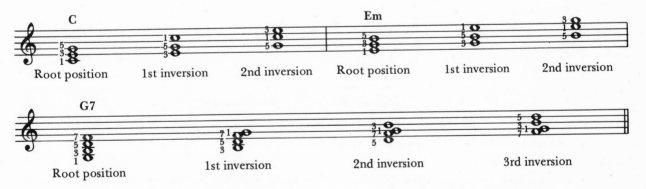

Even though inversions are named and are usually considered from the point of view of the lowest note our concern will be with the *highest*. That is because in our playing of melodies and chords up and down the neck of the banjo we shall be primarily involved with the notes as they fall on the first string—that is, the highest note of each chord.

The following diagrams represent movable chords (inversions) which may be played at any fret. The first diagram of each set is the original, first position, open-string formation of the chord. It is given here just to show you where the movable formation comes from. The chords will be named by inversion according to the standard terminology *but* our focus will be on the highest, not the lowest note. (Since a major chord is made up of three notes only the first three strings are necessary in forming the complete chord. The fourth string is included just to round out the fingering.)

When 5 is the highest note the chord is in root position. (Root position = 1,3,5.)

When 1 is the highest note the chord is in first inversion. (First inversion = 3,5,1.)

When 3 is the highest note the chord is in second inversion. (Second inversion = 5,1,3.)

Inversions of Major Chords—G Tuning

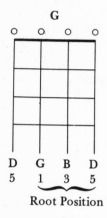

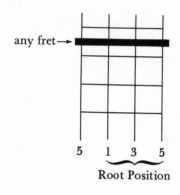

Special Open 4th String Positions

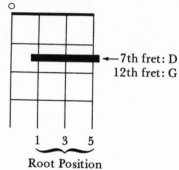

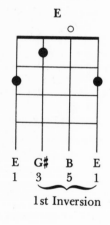

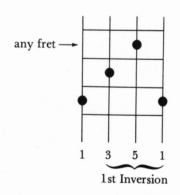

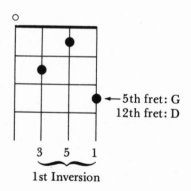

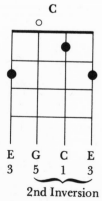

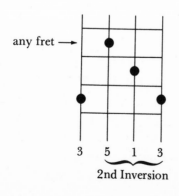

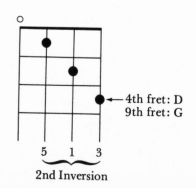

These diagrams are to be used as follows:

1. To play familiar chords in different positions.

Example: How many ways can you play a G chord? According to the table of major chords the notes of a G chord are G,B,D. Find these three notes on the first string. (See page 147 if you are not sure where they are.) Each of these frets represents a point at which one of the inversions may be played. Now you have to make the connection between G(1) and its inversion, B(3) and its inversion and D(5) and its inversion.

When G is the highest note the chord is in the first inversion. When B is the highest note the chord is in the second inversion. When D is the highest note the chord is in root position.

Find the three inversions of C and F.

2. To find "new" chords in different positions.

Example: How many different ways can you play an A-flat chord? Look up the notes in the table. Find those notes on the first string. Play the proper inversions at those frets as you did with the G chord.

Find the three inversions of C, Bb, E, . . . etc.

3. To play melodies and chords at the same time. This is, perhaps, the most important and most difficult skill to develop. But this is precisely where we have been heading in this chapter. In the two prior examples we have gone from the chord to the note. Now we have to go from the note to the chord. In the end it amounts to the same thing but your thinking has to start from a different point.

Example: You are playing a melody in G on the first string. The music tells you you must play the note B. The chord called for at that point is G. What do you do? You find B on the first string. You check the table of chords and find out that B is the 3 of a G chord. You play the proper inversion at the proper fret.

When dealing with inversions of dominant-seventh chords, just remember that these chords have four notes and, hence, four inversions. Because of the fingering limitations of the banjo the strict order of notes for each inversion is not always possible to obtain. We will name them according to the lowest note but once again we are primarily concerned with the highest note and where it falls on the first string.

Inversions of Dominant-Seventh Chords—G Tuning

E7

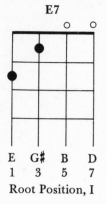

E	G♯	B	D
1	3	5	7

Root Position, I

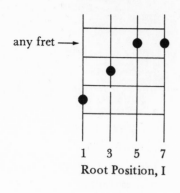

any fret →

| 1 | 3 | 5 | 7 |

Root Position, I

Special Open 4th String Positions

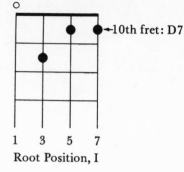

←10th fret: D7

| 1 | 3 | 5 | 7 |

Root Position, I

D7

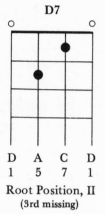

D	A	C	D
1	5	7	1

Root Position, II
(3rd missing)

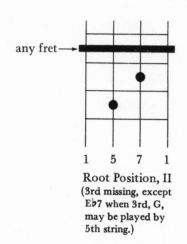

any fret →

| 1 | 5 | 7 | 1 |

Root Position, II
(3rd missing, except
E♭7 when 3rd, G,
may be played by
5th string.)

B7

D♯	A	B	D♯
3	7	1	3

1st Inversion
(5th missing)

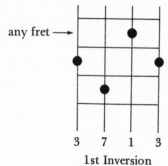

any fret →

| 3 | 7 | 1 | 3 |

1st Inversion
(5th missing, except
for C7 when 5th, G,
may be played by
5th string.)

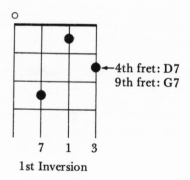

←4th fret: D7
9th fret: G7

7	1	3

1st Inversion

G7

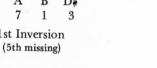

D	G	B	F
5	1	3	7

2nd Inversion

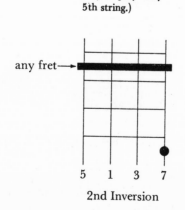

any fret →

| 5 | 1 | 3 | 7 |

2nd Inversion

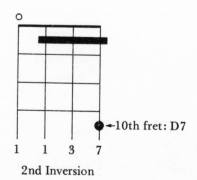

←10th fret: D7

| 1 | 1 | 3 | 7 |

2nd Inversion

106

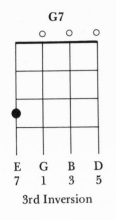

G7

E G B D
7 1 3 5

3rd Inversion

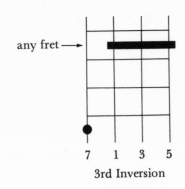

any fret →

7 1 3 5

3rd Inversion

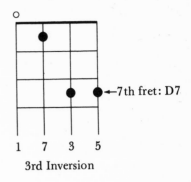

←7th fret: D7

1 7 3 5

3rd Inversion

Note that Root Position I and the 2nd Inversion both have the 7th on the 1st string. The choice of which pattern to use will depend upon what other patterns precede and follow this chord.

When playing a song using these inversions you may leave the fourth string (D) open while the G and D7 (or D) chords are sounding. This will make it a little easier to move around.

The following songs have been written an octave higher than "normal" in order that the melody notes fall on the first string. When playing other songs in this manner you may have to transpose mentally up an octave.

Skip to My Lou

Instrumental, Using Movable Inversions

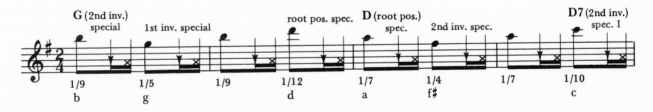

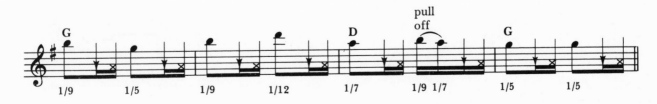

Boil Them Cabbage Down I

Instrumental, Using Movable Inversions

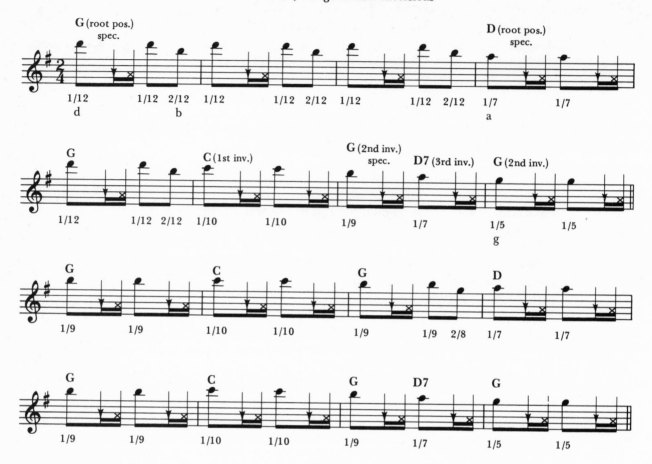

Boil Them Cabbage Down II

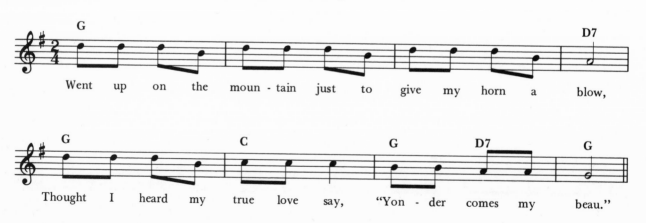

Went up on the moun - tain just to give my horn a blow,

Thought I heard my true love say, "Yon - der comes my beau."

Boil them cab - bage down, down, Turn them hoe - cakes 'round; The

on - ly song that I can sing is boil them cab - bage down.

G
Took my gal to a blacksmith shop
D7
To have her mouth made small.
G   C
She turned around a time or two
G   D7   G
And swallowed shop and all. *Chorus*

G
'Possum in a 'simmon tree,
D7
Raccoon on the ground.
G   C
Raccoon says, "You son-of-a-gun,
G   D7   G
Shake some 'simmons down!" *Chorus*

G
Someone stole my old 'coon dog,
D7
Wish they'd bring him back.
G   C
He chased the big hogs through the fence,
G   D7   G
The little ones through the crack. *Chorus*

G
Met a 'possum in the road,
D7
Blind as he could be.
G   C
Jumped the fence and whipped my dog
G   D7   G
And bristled up at me. *Chorus*

C Tuning

Inversions in the C tuning are essentially the same as in the G tuning, except for the different note on the fourth (C) string. When playing a song using these inversions you may leave the fourth string open while the C and F chords are sounding.

Inversions of Major Chords—C Tuning

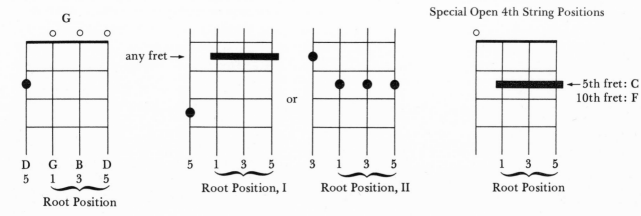

109

Inversions of Major Chords—C Tuning

F

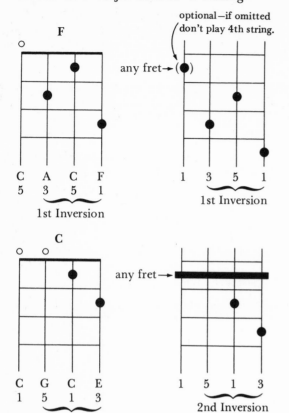

optional—if omitted
don't play 4th string.

any fret→

C A C F
5 3 5 1
1st Inversion

1 3 5 1
1st Inversion

C

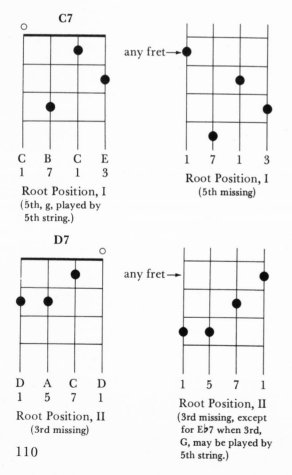

any fret→

C G C E
1 5 1 3
2nd Inversion

1 5 1 3
2nd Inversion

Special Open 4th String Positions

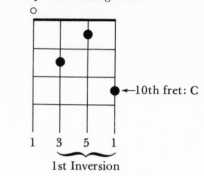

←10th fret: C

1 3 5 1
1st Inversion

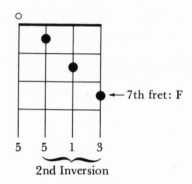

←7th fret: F

5 5 1 3
2nd Inversion

Inversions of Dominant-Seventh Chords—C Tuning

C7

any fret→

C B C E
1 7 1 3
Root Position, I
(5th, g, played by
5th string.)

1 7 1 3
Root Position, I
(5th missing)

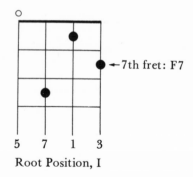

←7th fret: F7

5 7 1 3
Root Position, I

D7

any fret→

D A C D
1 5 7 1
Root Position, II
(3rd missing)

1 5 7 1
Root Position, II
(3rd missing, except
for E♭7 when 3rd,
G, may be played by
5th string.)

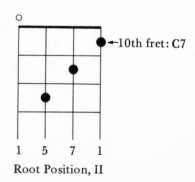

←10th fret: C7

1 5 7 1
Root Position, II

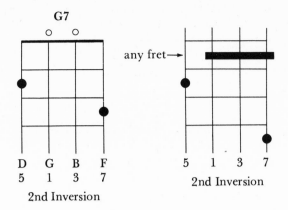

G7

D G B F
5 1 3 7

2nd Inversion

5 1 3 7

2nd Inversion

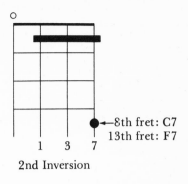

←8th fret: C7
13th fret: F7

1 3 7

2nd Inversion

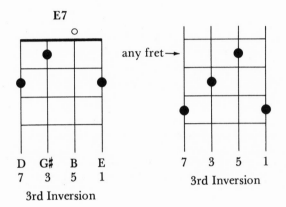

E7

D G# B E
7 3 5 1

3rd Inversion

7 3 5 1

3rd Inversion

This is the *only* instance where it is possible to get the 5th on the 1st string. It is physically impossible to get this inversion with any other chord at any other fret. If a 5th is called for in any dominant-seventh chord other than C7 play the root position major chord instead.

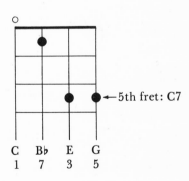

←5th fret: C7

C Bb E G
1 7 3 5

Note that Root Position II and the 3rd Inversion both have the 1st on the 1st string. The choice of which pattern to use will depend upon what other patterns precede and follow this chord.

The Cumberland Mountain Deer Chase I

Instrumental, Using Movable Inversions

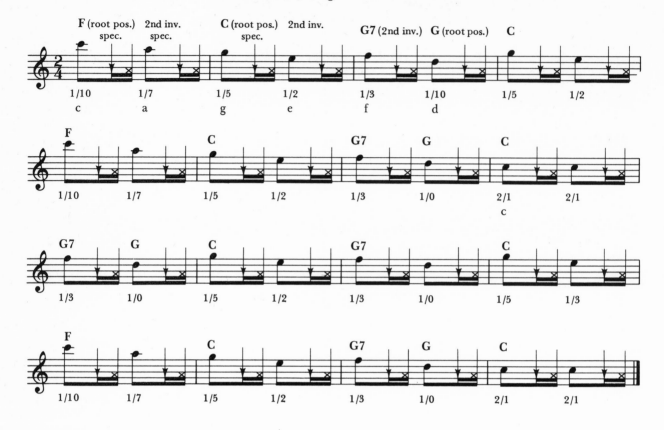

The Cumberland Mountain Deer Chase II

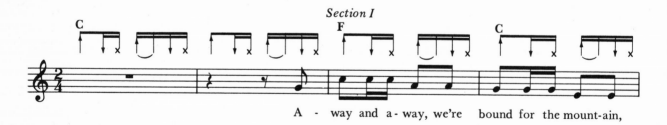

A - way and a - way, we're   bound for the mount-ain,

bound   for   the mount - ain,   bound   for   the mount - ain,   O - ver   the   fields   and   the

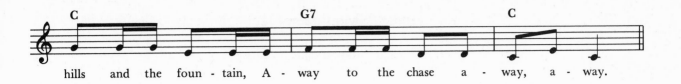

hills   and the foun - tain, A - way   to the chase a - way,   a - way.

Section II

Lis - ten to the hound dogs' heav - y   bay, Sound - ing time   all   the way, A -

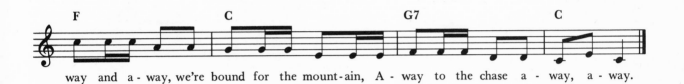

way and a - way, we're bound for the mount - ain, A - way to the chase a - way, a - way.

Sung to tune of Section II

G7   C
Rover, Rover, see him, see him,

G7   C
Rover, Rover, catch him, catch him,

 F   C
Away and away we're bound for the mountain,

 G7   C
Away to the chase, away, away.

Sung to tune of Section I

F   C
See there the wild deer, trembling panting,

G7   C
Trembling panting, trembling panting.

F   C
One moment pausing, no longer standing,

 G7   C
Away to the chase, away, away.

Repeat original section I

Home, Sweet Home I

Instrumental, Using Movable Inversions

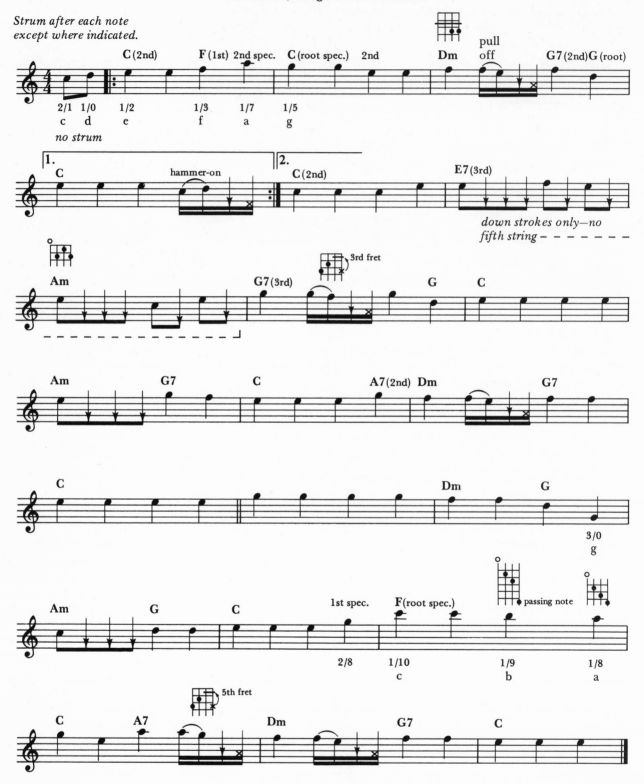

114

Home, Sweet Home II

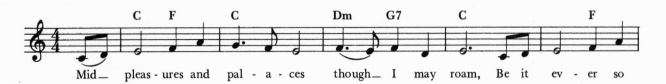

Mid — pleas - ures and pal - a - ces though— I may roam, Be it ev - er so

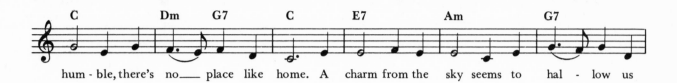

hum - ble, there's no— place like home. A charm from the sky seems to hal - low us

there, Which, seek through the world, is ne'er met— with else - where. Home! Home!—

Sweet, sweet home! There's— no place like home,— There's— no— place like home.

```
      C F     C              Dm G7     C
An exile from home, splendor dazzles in vain,
          F        C          Dm G7   C
Oh, give me my lowly thatched cottage again.
     E7         Am       G7          C
The birds singing gaily, that come at my call;
       Am   G7      C       A7   Dm G7    C
Give me them, with that peace of mind, dearer than all. Chorus


       C   F    C          Dm G7       C
To thee, I'll return overburdened with care,
            F       C          Dm  G7   C
The heart's dearest solace will smile on me there.
     E7          Am       G7        C
No more from that cottage again will I roam,
       AmG7    C      A7   Dm G7        C
Be it ever so humble, there's no place like home. Chorus
```

Inversions of Minor Chords—G Tuning

G♯m

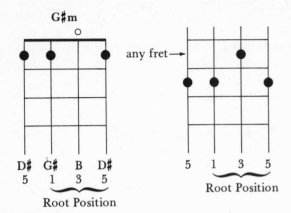

D♯ G♯   B   D♯
5   1   3   5

Root Position

any fret →

5   1   3   5

Root Position

Special Open 4th String Positions

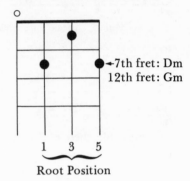

←7th fret: Dm
12th fret: Gm

1   3   5

Root Position

Em

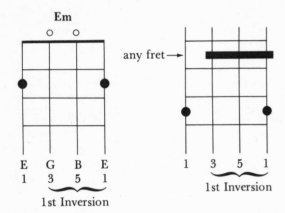

E   G   B   E
1   3   5   1

1st Inversion

any fret →

1   3   5   1

1st Inversion

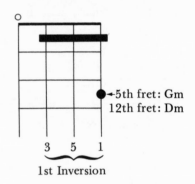

←5th fret: Gm
12th fret: Dm

3   5   1

1st Inversion

Cm

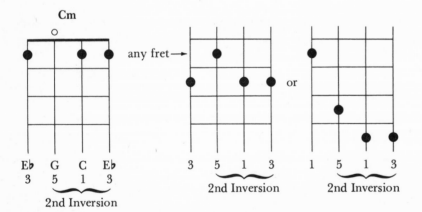

E♭   G   C   E♭
3   5   1   3

2nd Inversion

any fret →

3   5   1   3

2nd Inversion

or

1   5   1   3

2nd Inversion

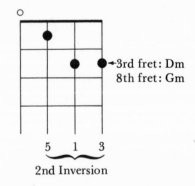

←3rd fret: Dm
8th fret: Gm

5   1   3

2nd Inversion

Deep Blue Sea I

Instrumental, Using Movable Inversions

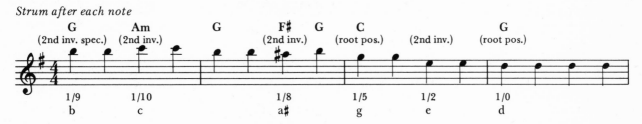

Deep Blue Sea II

Deep blue sea, ba-by, deep blue sea. Deep blue sea, ba-by,
deep blue sea. Deep blue sea, ba-by, deep blue sea.
It was Wil-lie what got drownd-ed In the deep blue sea.

G   Am G   C   G
Dig his grave with a silver spade,
      Am G   Am G D7
Dig his grave with a silver spade,
G   Am G   C   G
Dig his grave with a silver spade,

      It was Willie what got drownded
      C Cm G   D7   G
      In the deep blue sea.

G   Am G   C   G
Lower him down with a golden chain,
      Am G   Am G D7
Lower him down with a golden chain,
G   Am G   C   G
Lower him down with a golden chain,

      It was Willie what got drownded
      C Cm G   D7   G
      In the deep blue sea.

      G   Am G   C   G
      Golden sun bring him back again,
         Am G   Am G D7
      Golden sun bring him back again,
      G   Am G   C   G
      Golden sun bring him back again,

         It was Willie what got drownded
         C Cm G   D7   G
         In the deep blue sea. *Repeat verse one*

Inversions of Minor Chords—C Tuning

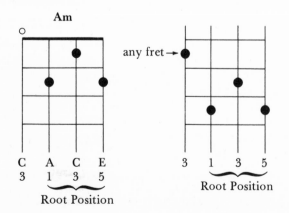

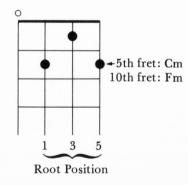

118

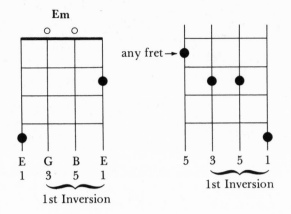

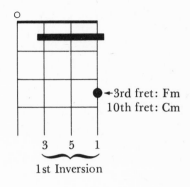

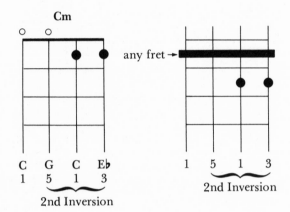

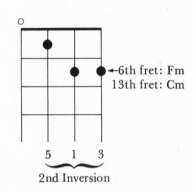

In the Garden

Instrumental, Using Movable Inversions

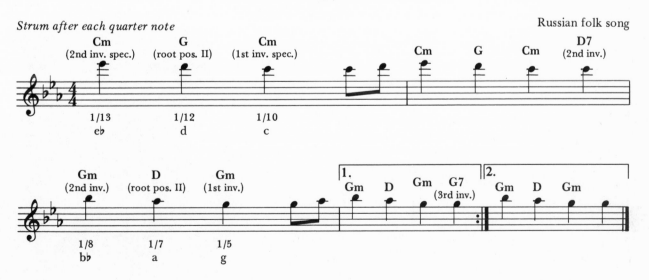

G Minor Tuning

Inversions in the G minor tuning are essentially the same as in the G tuning, except for the different note on the second (B♭) string. Here, too, you may leave the fourth string open while playing any G or D chord—minor, major or seventh.

Inversions of Minor Chords—G Minor Tuning

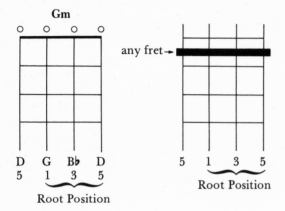

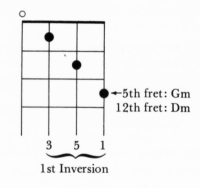

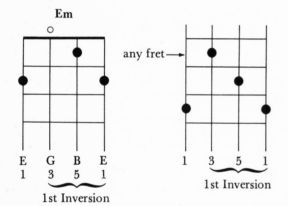

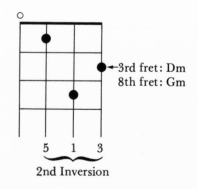

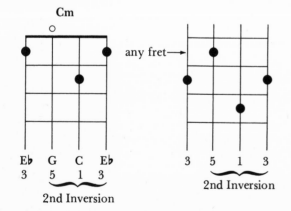

Inversions of Major Chords—G Minor Tuning

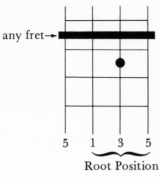

Special Open 4th String Positions

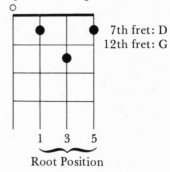

7th fret: D
12th fret: G

Root Position

G

D G B D
5 1 3 5

Root Position

any fret →

5 1 3 5

Root Position

1 3 5

Root Position

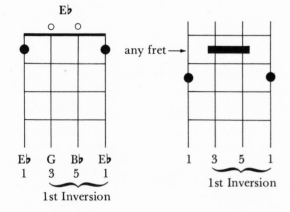

E♭

E♭ G B♭ E♭
1 3 5 1

1st Inversion

any fret →

1 3 5 1

1st Inversion

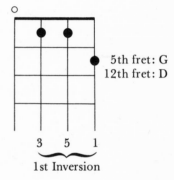

5th fret: G
12th fret: D

3 5 1

1st Inversion

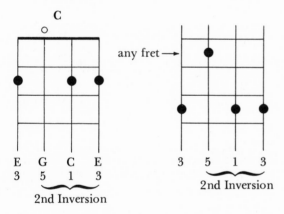

C

E G C E
3 5 1 3

2nd Inversion

any fret →

3 5 1 3

2nd Inversion

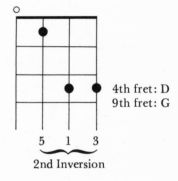

4th fret: D
9th fret: G

5 1 3

2nd Inversion

Inversions of Dominant-Seventh Chords—G Minor Tuning

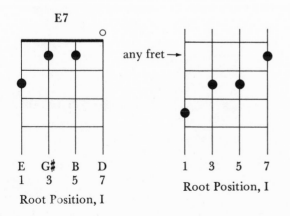

E7

E G♯ B D
1 3 5 7

Root Position, I

any fret →

1 3 5 7

Root Position, I

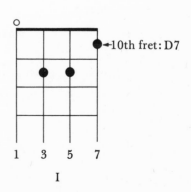

10th fret: D7

1 3 5 7

I

Inversions of Dominant-Seventh Chords—G Minor Tuning

D7

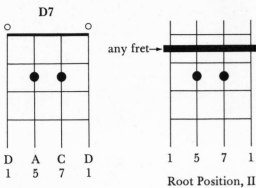

D A C D
1 5 7 1

Root Position, II
(3rd missing)

any fret→

1 5 7 1

Root Position, II
(3rd missing, except
for Eb7 when 3rd,
G, may be played by
5th string.)

Bb7

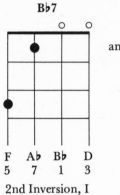

F Ab Bb D
5 7 1 3

2nd Inversion, I

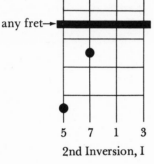

any fret→

5 7 1 3

2nd Inversion, I

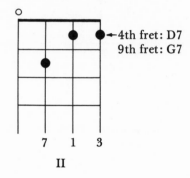

←4th fret: D7
9th fret: G7

7 1 3

II

G7

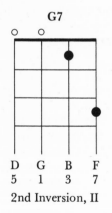

D G B F
5 1 3 7

2nd Inversion, II

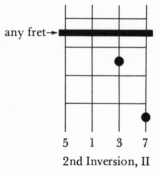

any fret→

5 1 3 7

2nd Inversion, II

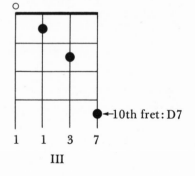

←10th fret: D7

1 1 3 7

III

G7

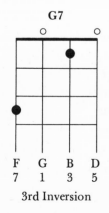

F G B D
7 1 3 5

3rd Inversion

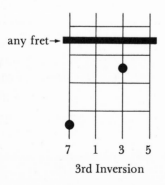

any fret→

7 1 3 5

3rd Inversion

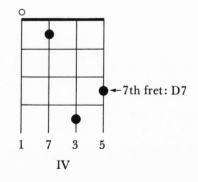

←7th fret: D7

1 7 3 5

IV

122

Hey, Ho, Nobody Home I

Instrumental, Using Movable Inversions

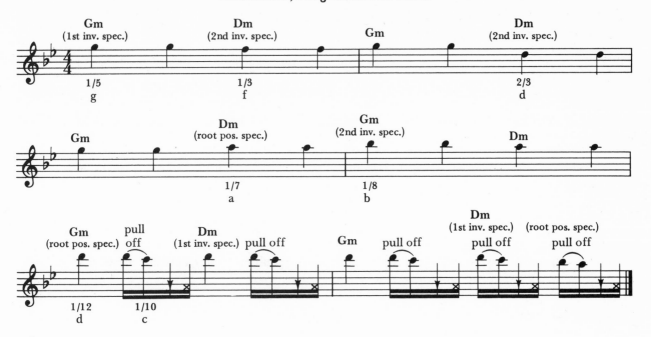

Hey, Ho, Nobody Home II

3-Part Round—Voices enter every two measures

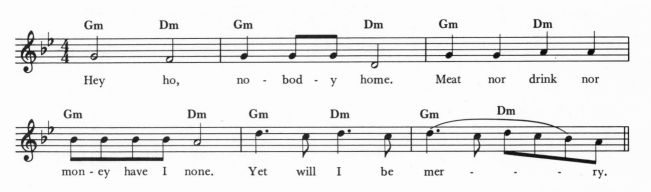

Songs are not usually written out so that the notes fall on the first string as they have been in this chapter. Normally they are written in registers which confine them to the open strings and the first few frets of each string. This means that in the practical application of all this information to future material you will generally have to transpose the melodies up an octave. Most banjoists, of course, are not concerned about reading the notes but play all their tunes by ear. This is what you should strive for as well. Banjo tunes and songs played on the banjo generally do not contain more than three chords. Some have more, naturally, but the point is that you will be playing the same inversions over and over again in the various tunings to such an extent that you will soon begin to "feel" just where the chords have to go. Once you get that feel you're all set!

CHAPTER SEVEN

MORE ON TECHNIQUE–RIGHT AND LEFT HANDS

We have spent quite a bit of time in the last two chapters discussing the ins and outs of chords and keys. As we turn our attention back to the actual technique of playing the banjo we will assume that you can decide for yourself where to place the capo to suit your voice, when to transpose to another key and tuning, and how to find any chord that you may be called upon to play. If any of these items still causes you trouble, do not hesitate to refer back to appropriate table, diagram or explanation.

Double-Thumbing

The right thumb is not totally restricted to the fifth string. In *double-thumbing* it moves back and forth from the fifth to either the second or third strings while the index finger plucks the first string on alternate beats.

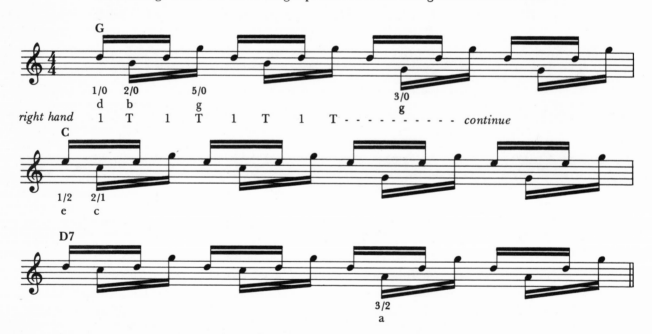

This pattern may be played in alternation with the basic strum. The double-thumbing segment takes the same amount of time as the basic strum.

Play all your songs from here on with chord inversions in various positions.

Sail Away, Ladies

If ev-er I get my new house done,

Sail a-way, la-dies, sail a-way, I'll give my old one to my son,

Sail a-way, la-dies, sail a-way. Don't she rock 'em die-dee-o, Don't she rock 'em,

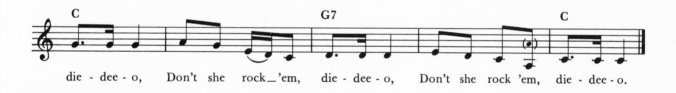

die-dee-o, Don't she rock—'em, die-dee-o, Don't she rock 'em, die-dee-o.

C   G7   C
Children, don't you grieve and cry,
             G7   C
  Sail away, ladies, sail away,
                  G7   C
You're gonna be angels by and by,
             G7   C
  Sail away, ladies, sail away. *Chorus*

C   G7   C
Come along, girls, and go with me,
             G7   C
  Sail away, ladies, sail away,
             G7   C
We'll go back to Tennessee,
             G7   C
  Sail away, ladies, sail away. *Chorus*

C   G7   C
I got a letter from Shiloh town,
             G7   C
  Sail away, ladies, sail away,
                G7   C
Big St. Louie is a-burning down,
             G7   C
  Sail away, ladies, sail away. *Chorus*

C   G7   C
I chew my tobacco and I spit my juice,
             G7   C
  Sail away, ladies, sail away,
                      G7   C
I love my own daughter but it ain't no use,
             G7   C
  Sail away, ladies, sail away. *Chorus*

I Was Born about Ten Thousand Years Ago

I was born a-bout ten thou-sand years a-go, There ain't

noth-ing in the world that I don't know. I saw Pe-ter, Paul and Mos-es play-ing

ring a-round the ros-es, And I'll whip the guy that says it is-n't so.

      G   D7
I saw Satan when he looked the Garden o'er,

                         G
I saw Eve and Adam driven from the door.

       C   G
From behind the bushes peeping seen the apple they was eating,

     D7   G
And I'll swear that I'm the guy what ate the core.

      G   D7
I taught Samson how to use his mighty hands,

                         G
Showed Columbus how to reach this happy land.

      C   G
And for Pharaoh's little kiddies built all the pyramiddies,

     D7   G
And to Sahara carried all the sand.

      G   D7
I taught Solomon his little ABC's,

                         G
And was the first to eat Limburger cheese.

      C   G
And while sailing down the bay with Methuselah one day,

     D7   G
I saved his flowing whiskers from the breeze.

        G   D7

Queen Elizabeth fell dead in love with me.

                              G

We were married in Milwaukee secretly.

      C   G

But I snuck around and shook 'er, to go with General Hooker,

     D7   G

To fight mosquiters down in Tennessee. *Repeat verse one.*

Go back and play some of your old songs with double-thumbing.

Frailing

Frailing is a variation of the basic strum. Rhythmically, it is identical with it. Physically, there is one important difference. The first beat—instead of being played with an upstroke of the index finger—is played with a hard downstroke of the nail of the second finger. This gives a rather percussive effect which is useful in ensembles when you want the banjo to be heard clearly.

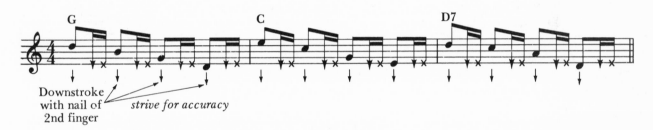

Downstroke with nail of 2nd finger   *strive for accuracy*

You can try any of your songs with frailing. Incidentally, you don't have to play a whole song with the same strum. You can start with the basic strum and add a little double-thumbing and frailing whenever you feel like it.

The Blues Shuffle

This strum is extremely useful in accompanying work songs, blues and other slower songs which do not lend themselves to the bouncy basic strum and its variations. It is composed of four brush strokes, as follows:

1. The nails of fingers 1, 2 and 3 strike the 5th and 4th strings in a loose-wrist, brushing movement.
2. Repeat.
3. The same fingernails brush down across all the strings.
4. Index finger brushes lightly upward over strings 1 and 2.

Rhythmically it looks like this:

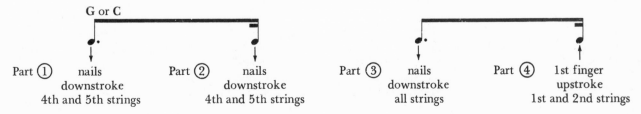

127

The notes which ordinarily would be hammered-on may be added at Part 3 of the strum. This is not a hammer-on. Play the notes in the "normal" manner.

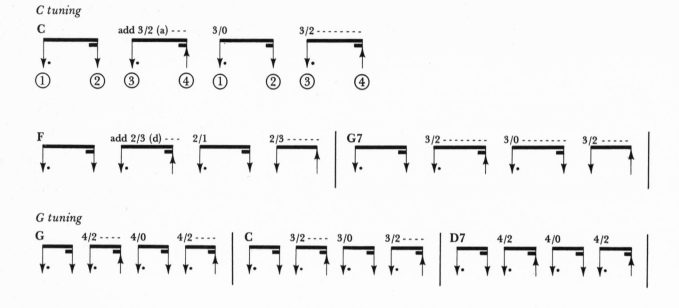

The Midnight Special

Blues shuffle   *Verse*

Well, you wake up in the morn - ing,_____
ta - ble,_____

continue

_____ Hear the ding - dong ring._____ you go march - ing to the
_____ knife and fork and a pan,_____ If you say a thing a -

ta - ble,_____ See the same__ damn__ thing. Well, it's on a one__
bout it,_____ You're in trou - ble with the

man. Let the Mid-night Spe-cial_____ shine her light_____ on me,_____

_____ Let the Mid-night Spe-cial_____ shine her ev-er-lov-in' light on me.__

G   C   G
Now, if you ever go to Houston, Lord, you better walk right,

     D7   G
And you better not stagger, yes, you better not fight.

       C   G
'Cause the sheriff will arrest you, and he'll carry you down—

       D7   G
You can bet your bottom dollar you're penitentiary bound. *Chorus*

G   C   G
Yonder comes Miss Rosie. Tell me how do you know?

     D7   G
I know her by her apron and the dress she wore.

      C   G
Umberella on her shoulder, piece of paper in her hand.

      D7   G
Well, I heard her tell the captain, "Turn a-loose my man." *Chorus*

G   C   G
Lord, Thelma said she loved me, but I believe she told a lie,

      D7   G
'Cause she hasn't been to see me since last July.

      C   G
Well, she brought me little coffee and she brought me little tea,

      D7   G
She brought me nearly everything except the jailhouse key. *Chorus*

G   C   G
I'm goin' away to leave you, and my time it ain't long.

      D7   G
The man is gonna call me and I'm goin' home.

      C   G
Then I'll be done all my grievin', whoopin', hollerin' and cryin',

      D7   G
Then I'll be done all my studyin' about my great long time. *Chorus*

Take This Hammer

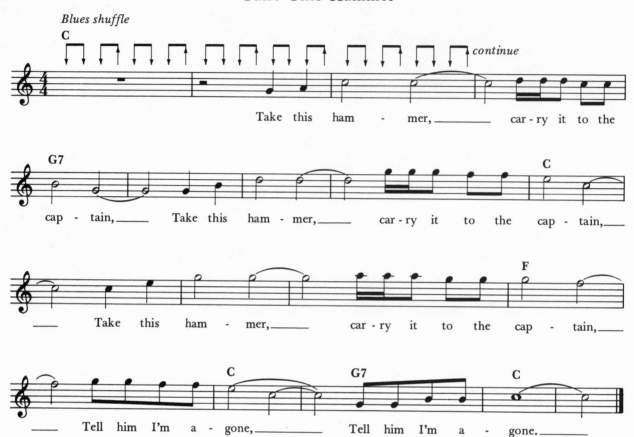

Blues shuffle

Take this ham - mer, _____ car-ry it to the cap - tain, _____ Take this ham-mer, _____ car-ry it to the cap - tain, _____ Take this ham - mer, _____ car-ry it to the cap - tain, _____ Tell him I'm a - gone, _____ Tell him I'm a - gone. _____

        C   G7
If he asks you, was I laughing,
        C
If he asks you, was I laughing,
        F
If he asks you, was I laughing,
        C   G7   C
Tell him I was crying, tell him I was crying.

        C   G7
If he asks you, was I running,
        C
If he asks you, was I running,
        F
If he asks you, was I running,
        C   G7   C
Tell him I was flying, tell him I was flying.

        C   G7
I don't want no cornbread and molasses,
                      G7
I don't want no cornbread and molasses,
                      F
I don't want no cornbread and molasses,
        C   G7   C
They hurt my pride, they hurt my pride.

C G7
I don't want no cold iron shackles,
C
I don't want no cold iron shackles,
F
I don't want no cold iron shackles,
C G7 C
Around my leg, around my leg. *Repeat verse one*

Finger-Picking—Bluegrass Style

Finger-picking is a general term which refers to the playing of the notes of a chord one at a time rather than all at once. In another context we would call this technique "arpeggios."

There are many patterns which can be developed in finger-picking. Most of these involve the thumb and the first two fingers. As a warm-up exercise try this "endless" series.

G tuning

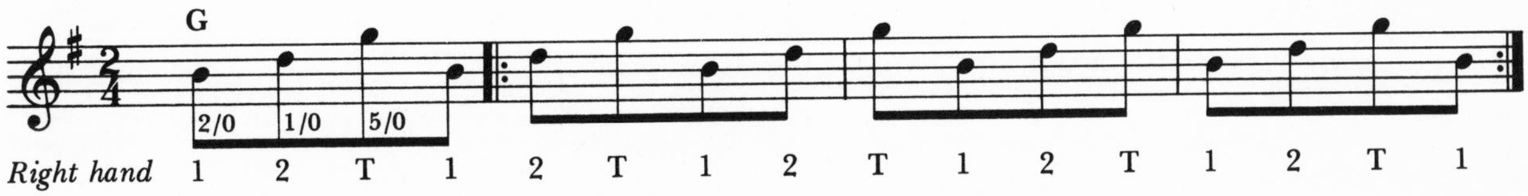

To get a feeling of "beginning and end" we must make the following change:

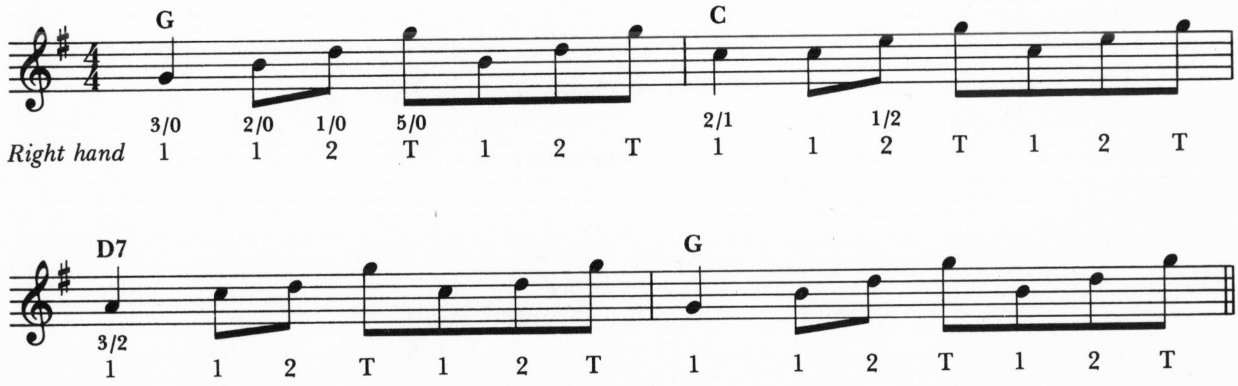

Wildwood Flower

Finger Picking

I will twine and will min - gle my rav - en black hair, With the ros - es so red and the lil - ies so fair. The myr - tle so green of an em - er - ald hue, The pale em - an - i - ta. and is - lip so blue.

           G   D7   G
Oh, he promised to love me, he promised to love

                                    D7   G
And to cherish me always all others above.

                              C   G
I woke from my dream and my idol was clay,

                             D7   G
My passion for loving had vanished away.

           G   D7   G
Oh, he taught me to love him, he called me his flower,

                             D7   G
A blossom to cheer him through life's weary hour.

                      C   G
But now he is gone and left me alone,

                           D7   G
The wild flowers to weep and the wild birds to mourn.

           G   D7   G
I will dance and I'll sing and my heart shall be gay,

                             D7   G
I will charm every heart in the crowd I survey.

                             C   G
Though my heart now is breaking, he never shall know,

                           D7   G
How his name makes me tremble, my pale cheeks to glow.

           G   D7   G
I will dance and I'll sing and my heart shall be gay.

                           D7   G
I will banish this weeping, drive troubles away.

                         C   G
I will live yet to see him regret this dark hour,

                         D7   G
When he won and neglected this frail wildwood flower.

The thumb can drop down to the third or fourth string.

Try "Wildwood Flower" again with the thumb moving in this manner.

Dissonant and non-chordal notes may be added to the patterns on various strings.

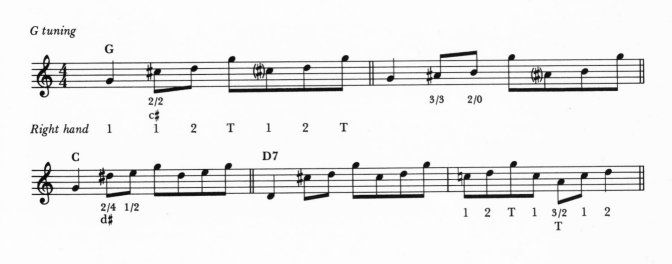

133

Often these notes are hammered-on up to a unison with the next higher open string.

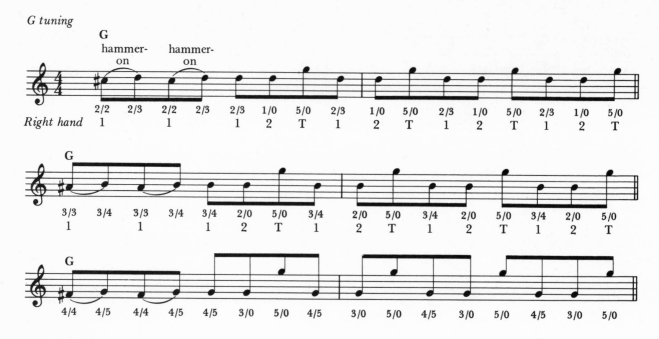

Sprinkle some of these added notes throughout "John Henry."

John Henry I

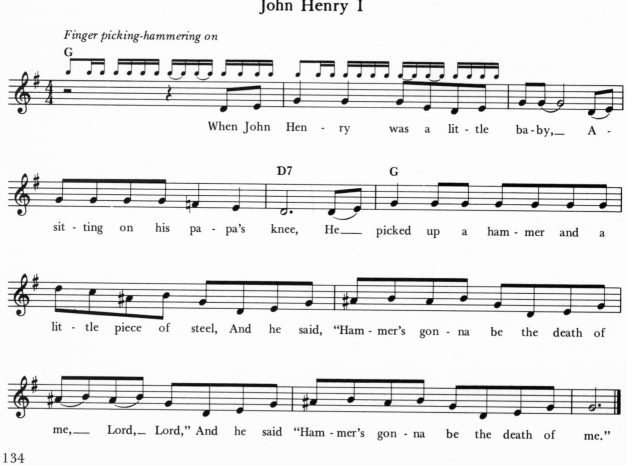

Finger picking-hammering on

When John Hen - ry was a lit - tle ba - by,__ A -

sit - ting on his pa - pa's knee, He__ picked up a ham - mer and a

lit - tle piece of steel, And he said, "Ham - mer's gon - na be the death of

me,__ Lord,__ Lord," And he said "Ham - mer's gon - na be the death of me."

Well, the captain said to John Henry,
G

"Gonna bring that steel drill 'round.
D7

Gonna bring that steam drill out on the job,
G

Gonna whup that steel on down, Lord, Lord,

Gonna whup that steel on down."

John Henry said to his captain,
G

"A man ain't nothing but a man,
D7

And before I'd let that steam drill beat me down,
G

I'll die with a hammer in my hand, Lord, Lord,

I'll die with a hammer in my hand."

John Henry said to his shaker,
G

"Shaker, why don't you sing?
D7

I'm a-throwing twelve pounds from my hips on down,
G

Just listen to that cold steel ring, Lord, Lord,

Listen to that cold steel ring."

John Henry said to his shaker,
G

"Shaker, why don't you pray?
D7

'Cause if I miss this little piece of steel,
G

Tomorrow be your burying day, Lord, Lord,

Tomorrow be your burying day."

John Henry was driving on the mountain,
G

And his hammer was flashing fire.
D7

And the last words I heard that poor boy say,
G

"Gimme a cool drink of water 'fore I die, Lord, Lord,

Gimme a cool drink of water 'fore I die."

John Henry, he drove fifteen feet,
G

The steam drill only made nine.
D7

But he hammered so hard that he broke his poor heart,
G

And he laid down his hammer and he died, Lord, Lord,

He laid down his hammer and he died.

They took John Henry to the graveyard,
G

And they buried him in the sand.
D7

And every locomotive comes a-roaring by, says,
G

"There lies a steel-driving man, Lord, Lord,

There lies a steel-driving man."

Playing melody in the finger-picking style involves a great deal of imagination and flexibility. You simply cannot get locked into an unchanging pattern with your fingers if you hope to be able to bring out the tune. You have to be ready and able to break the pattern whenever the melody demands it. That may mean changing strings or fingers in midstream. The difficult thing is that one cannot predict at the outset of a piece what departures from the pattern may be encountered from measure to measure. You have to take each new situation as you come to it and figure out a new solution every time.

"John Henry" is a good tune to examine from this point of view.

John Henry II

Instrumental

CHAPTER EIGHT

INSTRUMENTAL SOLOS

A good banjo player should be able to play the tune of any song he can sing—in any style of his choosing. It was to this end that we discussed the question of movable inversions, for the melody can lead us up and down the neck of the banjo.

The basic banjo strum and frailing, with their clearly accentuated first beat, are also indispensable tools in the playing of melodies.

Finger-picking is another, more complex, approach to this problem.

Putting all these elements together into a coherent finished product—a well-executed instrumental solo—requires diligent work over a long period of time.

The instrumentals presented here, in various styles, will serve both as a review of what you have learned to date and a jumping-off point for your own future development.

The Slide

We need to learn one more bit of technique at this time, the *slide.* As the name implies, a finger of the left hand slides from one fret to another after the right hand has played the initial note.

Old Joe Clark I

Basic strum, pulling-off, hammering-on

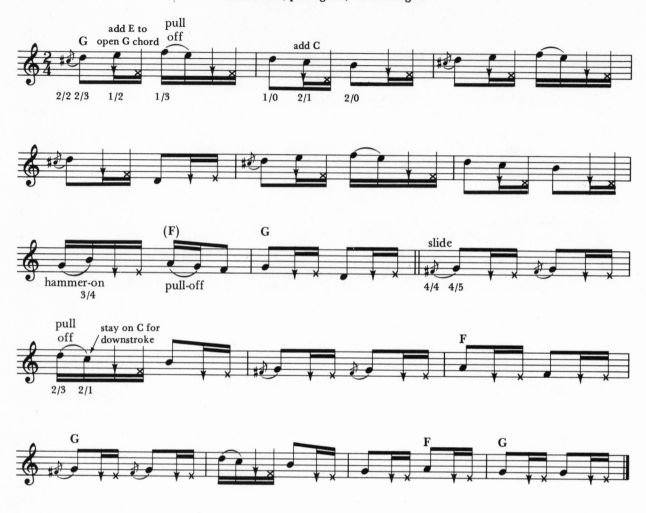

Old Joe Clark II

Finger-picking

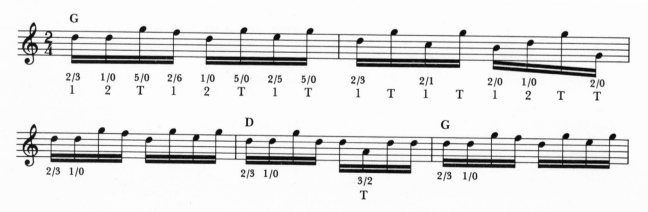

138

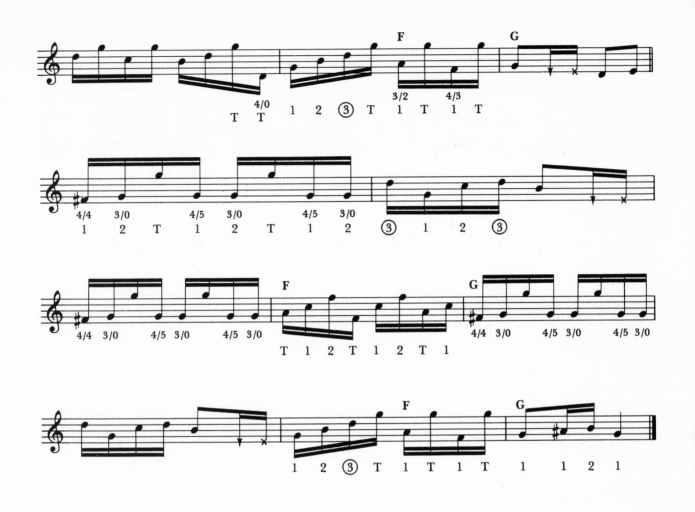

Cripple Creek I

Basic strum or frailing, hammering-on, pulling-off, slides.

Cripple Creek II

Finger-picking

Right hand

Cindy I

Basic strum, pulling-off, hammering-on

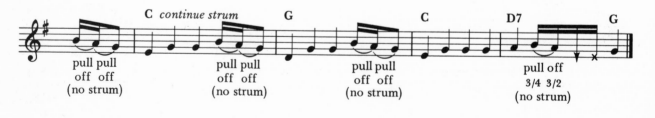

Cindy II

Finger-picking, pulling-off

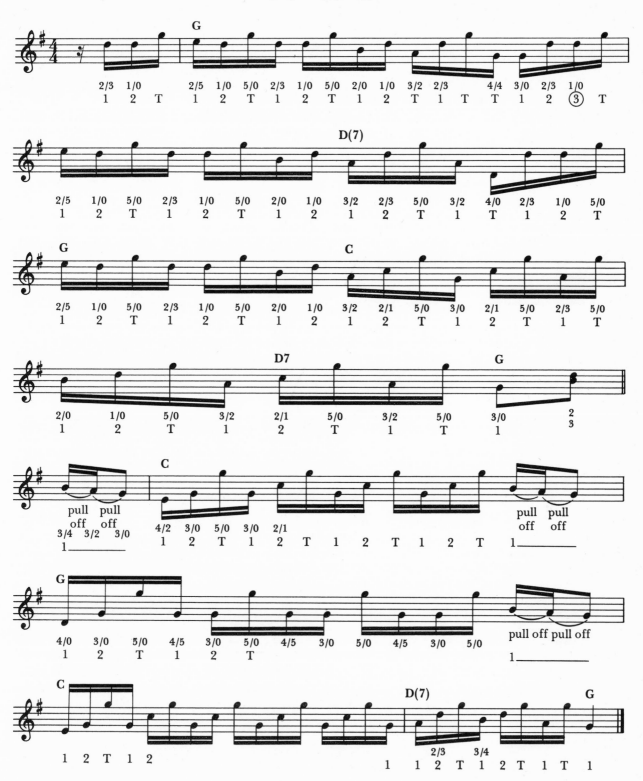

Arkansas Traveler

Basic strum, double-thumbing, hammering-on, pulling-off

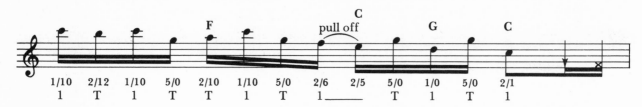

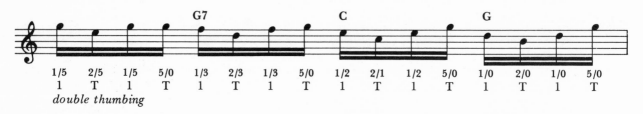

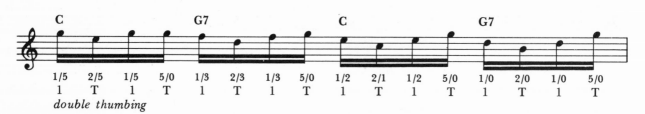

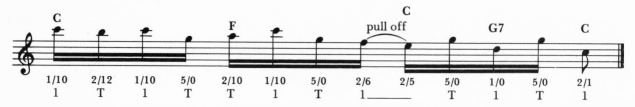

Wildwood Flower

Finger-picking, slide

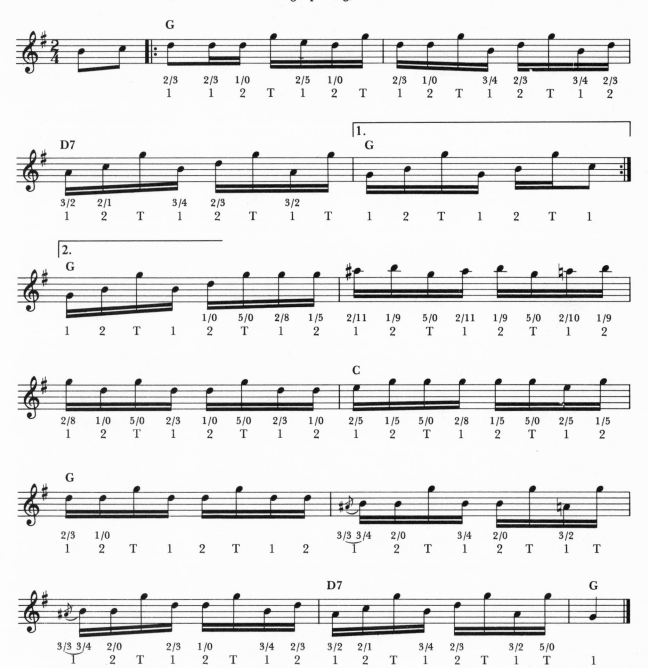

CHAPTER NINE
NOTE READING

C Tuning

Notes On the C (fourth) string:

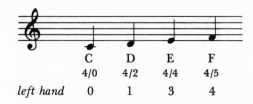

	C	D	E	F
	4/0	4/2	4/4	4/5
left hand	0	1	3	4

Exercise:

Notes On the G (third) string:

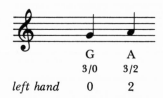

	G	A
	3/0	3/2
left hand	0	2

Exercise:

Notes On the B (second) string:

B   C
2/0   2/1
left hand   0   1

Exercise:

Notes On the D (first) string:

D   E   F   G
1/0 1/2 1/3 1/5
left hand   0   2   3   5

Exercise:

C Major scale:

G Tuning

The difference between the C and G tunings is, of course, the changing fourth string—from C to D. The difference between the *key* of C and the *key* of G lies in the appearance of the note F-sharp in the key of G. The key of C has no sharps or flats in its scale.

Notes On the D (fourth) string:

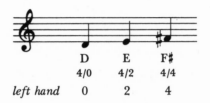

Exercise:

The notes on the G and B strings are the same as in the C tuning.

Notes On the D (first) string:

Exercise:

G Major Scale

146

Chromatic Scale—C Tuning

C	C#	Db	D	D#	Eb	E	Fb	E#	F	F#	Gb	G	G#	Ab	A	A#	Bb	B	Cb	B#	C
4/0	4/1		4/2	4/3		4/4		4/5		4/6		3/0	3/1		3/2	3/3		2/0		2/1	

C#	Db	D	D#	Eb	E	Fb	E#	F	F#	Gb	G	G#	Ab	A	A#	Bb	B	Cb	B#	C	C#	Db	D	*etc.*
2/2		1/0	1/1		1/2		1/3		1/4		1/5	1/6		1/7	1/8		1/9		1/10		1/11		1/2	

Chromatic Scale—G Tuning

Only the D (fourth) string presents a new series of notes.

D	D#	Eb	E	Fb	E#	F	F#	Gb
4/0	4/1		4/2		4/3		4/4	

147

CHAPTER TEN

TUNING AND RETUNING

All string instruments must be constantly tuned by their players. Perhaps no other instrument requires such constant attention in this respect as the five-string banjo. For, not only does it get out of tune in the natural course of events (like a violin or guitar), but, as you know, its tuning itself is not constant from key to key.

A banjo may be tuned by a number of different means.

Tuning to a Piano

The notes of a banjo sound one octave (eight notes) lower than they are written. This in no way affects your playing—it is just something to keep in mind as you compare the notes of the open strings to the corresponding notes on a piano.

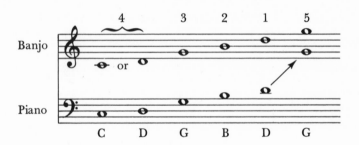

Tuning to a Guitar

Since banjos are often played in conjunction with guitars here is how your guitarist friends can help you tune up.

Notes on the Guitar Which Correspond to Open Strings on the Banjo:

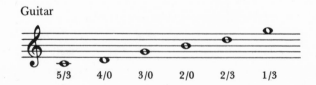

Tuning the Banjo Relative to Itself

If you do not happen to have a piano or guitarist handy you can still tune the banjo *relative to itself.* You have to make one initial assumption—that the fourth string (in whichever tuning you desire) is "more or less" where it should be. That "more or less" will become "more" as you gain experience with the passage of time. You have to have played the banjo for a while before you develop the sense of what an in-tune instrument sounds like.

Anyway, once you have decided that the fourth string is in tune—let's say in the G tuning—you proceed as follows:

- The fifth fret of the fourth (D) string is G. This is what the third string should sound like. Tune the third string to this note. Then . . .

- The fourth fret of the third (G) string is B. This is what the second string should sound like. Tune the second string to this note. Then . . .

- The third fret of the second (B) string is D. This is what the first string should sound like. Tune the first string to this note. Then . . .

- The fifth fret of the first (D) string is G. This is what the fifth string should sound like. Tune the fifth string to this note. Then . . .

- Check what you have done by slowly playing all the open strings. By now you should have some idea of what an in-tune G chord sounds like. If something sounds wrong, retune by this method. Don't be discouraged if it doesn't come out perfect the first (or second) time. It is essentially a process of trial and error. Your critical ear will develop as you tune again and again and again . . . .

In the C tuning . . . the seventh fret of the fourth (C) string is G . . . From here on you proceed as before.

After you have tuned up check it out by slowly playing a C chord.

The Long-Neck Banjo

Some brilliant ideas are essentially so simple that we marvel at them and wonder why somebody didn't think of them before. So it is with Pete Seeger and his "invention"—the long-neck banjo.

A long-neck banjo is a banjo with three extra frets added at the lower end of the neck—to your left as you hold it. This extension facilitates playing in certain awkward keys and also adds a deeper sonority to the instrument.

What is involved is simply this: Playing in the key of F in the C tuning is never satisfying because of the angling of the capo. F♯ (or G♭), while not the most commonly played key, still is occasionally needed to fit someone's vocal requirements for a particular song. To all intents and purposes, however, it is really not playable since it involves removing the capo and replacing the capo and replacing it on the far side of the fifth string peg.

Playing in certain minor keys also poses a problem. The minor keys in the C tuning (Cm, C♯m, Dm, E♭m, Em) are easier to work around in for most songs than those in the G or G minor tunings. But these five keys do not afford enough of a range for the average person to sing all the songs in minor keys that he might like. Particularly, the key of A minor—so popular with guitarists—never has quite the sonority in the G tuning that it should.

Also, since G is the preferred key for many square dance, hoedown, and bluegrass instrumentals, and since many of these songs are too high for the average voice to sing in G, this also poses a bit of a problem.

So what did Pete do? He had John D'Angelico, master guitar maker, graft three extra lower frets onto his banjo, and *voilà!*

Now in the C tuning he could play in the keys of B, B♭ and A major *and* minor. And in the G tuning he could play in the keys of F♯ (G♭), F and E.

And you can, too!

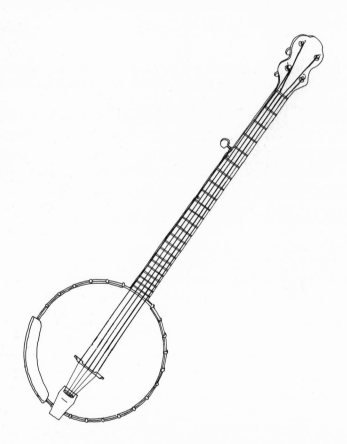